THE ANTIRACIST

HOW TO START THE CONVERSATION ABOUT RACE AND TAKE ACTION

KONDWANI FIDEL

FOREWORD BY DEVIN ALLEN

Hot Books

Hot Books may be purchased in bulk at special discounts for sales promotion, corporate gifts, fund-raising, or educational purposes. Special editions can also be created to specifications. For details, contact the Special Sales Department, Skyhorse Publishing, 307 West 36th Street, 11th Floor, New York, NY 10018 or info@skyhorsepublishing.com.

Hot Books® is a registered trademark of Skyhorse Publishing, Inc.®, a Delaware corporation.

Visit our website at www.skyhorsepublishing.com.

10 9 8 7 6 5 4 3 2 1

Library of Congress Cataloging-in-Publication Data is available on file.

Print ISBN: 978-1-5107-6420-0
Ebook ISBN: 978-1-5107-6421-7

Cover design by Kai Texel

Printed in the United States of America

CONTENTS

Wake up to a hunnit murders, go to sleep to glock nine's
Fireworks and lullabies, it ain't even Fourth of July
But what's independence, when you deprived of your innocence?
Fighting a life sentence before you can form sentences.
—Eddie Vanz

God Bless America, but bless my niggas too.
—Zadia

The first change that takes place is in your mind. You have to change your mind before you change the way you live and the way you move. The thing that's going to change people is something that nobody will ever be able to capture on film. It's just something that you see and you'll think, "Oh I'm on the wrong page," or "I'm on the right page but the wrong note. And I've got to get in sync with everyone else to find out what's happening in this country.
—Gil Scott Heron

Rebellion is nuanced.
Sometimes it looks like rage.
Sometimes it looks like love.
Sometimes it looks like silence.
Sometimes it's just existing
It's rebellion nonetheless.
—Erica Buddington

Foreword

I was born into a world heavily vested in the idea that people with Black skin have no voice; however, I was lucky enough to find my voice—even though I had no place to nurture, or express, it—and that is the reality for many Black artists in America.

Born and raised in West Baltimore during one of the deadliest eras of American history, surviving was more of a priority than art or the understanding of what it means. At the age of seventeen, I lost one of my close childhood friends, Lor Mar, to gun violence.

We met at the age of eight and did everything together. Lor Mar loved gambling more than anyone I ever knew, and it wasn't strange to see him with his head deep in a dice game around our neighborhood. An argument over a couple dollars had broken out during one of those games that ended with shots being fired from multiple directions and Lor Mar was caught in the middle—he died on the scene. Lor Mar was a great person, fresh out of high school, a soon-to-be father, and in the blink of an eye—gone. After his death, other people around me were murdered as well, so naturally, I thought I was going to meet that same demise.

Baltimore wears hard on bones, and we don't really get to be young or get lost in the joys of childhood. We often spend most of our formative years in hopelessness—told to go to school, get a job, and go to college. Keep your head down, obey the law, be an upstanding citizen, and trust the system. The sad reality is that you can do all of that, and still end up with a bullet in your head. But if you do survive, following the lessons most of us are taught hinders our creativity and growth, forcing us to subscribe to the same vicious cycle of nothingness that guarantees the same normalcy that existed before us. In the world that I was born in, being a Black artist was the exact opposite of that normalcy and always an unobtainable dream—mainly because our flames of creativity are smothered before they can even spread into our true potential.

I've always been an artist, but I never tapped into my talents until later in life, on a journey where I found my purpose. I remember sharing my dreams with my peers and telling people on the blocks that I was going to be a photographer, and them just making fun of my interest in becoming an artist—and it wasn't their fault since we really never knew any professional artist. They told me I had to go to one of those fancy White institutions to learn art and photography—"You can't pick it up and just do it," they said, especially as a Black man from the streets, because Black men from the streets aren't good enough. I ignored them, and with the help of YouTube and books by Gordon Parks, I proved all of them wrong.

Schools in Baltimore never taught me anything about Black artists. I read Langston Hughes maybe a few times, but my mom taught me about legends like Nina Simone, Gil Scott-Heron, Billie Holiday, and more. When I decided to be an artist, I had to look into the past to understand my future: what I would have to overcome, and how I could create my style and make my footprint in this world. In my process, I began studying Gordon Parks, Anthony Barbosa, and Jamal Shibez. Their work inspired me, and I started making a name for myself as an artist.

On April 12, 2015, Freddie Carlos Gray was arrested by Baltimore City police for nothing, handcuffed and thrown in the back of the paddy wagon headfirst, without being strapped in. Freddie never made it to jail. Instead, he ended up in Shock Trauma with severe injuries to his spinal cord, which would ultimately take his life on April 19. Being from West Baltimore, I have had my share of altercations with BCP, so watching this story unfold hit home because that could have been me. I know my city like the back of my hand, and after watching Ferguson unfold and how media poorly controlled the narrative around Mike Brown, I wanted to control our story. I went to every protest and town hall, documenting everything—the good, the bad, and everything in between—putting it all out on social media, so people could see what is really taking place in the streets of Baltimore. Because for far too long, our narrative had been controlled by external voices, phony activists with no city connections, fake reverends, and clowns who regularly ignore and disregard the real Baltimore.

The authenticity of my work allowed it to become its own driving force, spreading from my camera to the social media accounts of Rihanna, SZA, and Beyoncé all the way to the *New York Times*. And then *Time* magazine called, wanting me on the cover of their magazine as the third amateur photographer to do that in the history of the publication. I had finally found my voice.

Although I was excited that my art gained national recognition, I also felt conflicted because this opportunity grew from the death of Freddie Gray. But similar to Gordon Parks, my camera became my choice of weapon against "what I hated most about the universe: racism, intolerance, and poverty." I wanted to use my newfound platform to inspire and elevate other Black artists—and one of them was a talented kid from East Baltimore named Kondwani Fidel.

I remember coming across this video called "The Baltimore Bullet Train" that was raw, gritty, and spoke to my Baltimore, the streets I know. I'd never heard of Kondwani before, but his work changed me, and I had to find him—I was determined to work with him. The Baltimore art world is small, so it didn't take long for me to connect with this one artist who introduced us. I told him his poetry ran through my bones, because I lived the words that he was speaking. Everything this guy did with words, I had been doing with my camera, so I invited him to perform at "Wakenings In a New Light" at the Reginald F. Lewis Museum, my first exhibition centered on the Baltimore Uprising.

On the opening day in July 2015, Kondwani performed, and I got to see him live for the first time—I realized that I'd never felt that type of energy from a poet ever in my life. From that moment on, I knew he was something special.

He's able to bring out the sorrow, the rawness, and Baltimore's grittiness in the most beautiful, elegant way; one that you'll only capture if you've grown up in the city. James Baldwin once said that "to be a negro in this country is to be in a constant state of rage." We use art as our vehicle to release that rage, and I think Kondwani portrays that very well. In his poetry, his essays, and his speeches—you can feel the kind of rage and pain needed to educate the masses and spark real change.

Kondwani is a gem—literally, a rose growing from the concrete right before our eyes, as he owns his greatness while maintaining a humble spirit. Time and time again he's overcome every hurdle that life has thrown at him. And growing up in Baltimore, we're not just ducking bullets, fighting addictions and police, we are also fighting racism. The ugliest kind of racism that specializes in killing Black people.

As Black artists, we have an obligation to our community, and as artists, we become the voice, eyes, and ears for our people. We look to shed light where it hasn't gone before or been neglected for far too long. We must continuously grow, learn, and become better versions of ourselves so we can better serve our people. Being a true artist for the people comes with being able to make sacrifices, and at times, putting yourself last, and Kondwani understands that and it is ingrained in his work. So after the *Time* cover, I was back in the streets helping kids, and after my second *Time* cover, I'm still in the streets helping kids— and over the five years in between those covers, Kondwani has been right there by my side, inspiring those same young people, fighting the real fight.

So, when you read Kondwani's work, know that it is raw, authentic, pure, honest, and gives a voice that so many of us Black artists are denied or are in search of. And instead of using that voice to uplift himself, he's using it to explain how racism works, teach others how to be antiracist, and spread love to us all.

—Devin Allen

Introduction

He was just a kid.

Blue and red lights bouncing off of buildings and the faces of spectators, yellow tape that the police try to keep you behind. Broken glass lying on the curb from the bottle of Bud Ice that fell out of the kid's hand. There's a little boy out there, who's maybe two years old, laughing and stomping on the beer, as if it were a rain puddle.

The corner store clerk just finished closing up his shop, he's out there, reminiscing on the kid's transition: a toddler who went from toting stuffed Barney animals, purchasing honey buns and sunflower seeds for breakfast, which later got swapped out for alcohol and blunts.

There's a little girl who's around twelve years old, dressed in SpongeBob printed pajama pants, slippers, and a bonnet—her tears are crashing the concrete, she's screaming, "that's crazy, niggas be so quick to pick up a gun. Niggas are scared . . . don't even wanna fight no more." She doesn't realize that this kind of murder has nothing to do with "niggas being scared," it's just that niggas are not fools—niggas got tired of bringing scarred knuckles to gun wars.

There's someone's grandmother peeking out of window blinds, shaking her head in disgust. She's been on this Earth, in this neighborhood, all seventy years of her life—this isn't her first rodeo. Sending prayers to the Lord is the only formula she believes in to stop the chaos in the city.

There's a boy pacing back and forth, smoking a Newport down till it burns the filter—he's about fourteen. He has revenge on his tongue because the kid is someone who he looked up to, who he admired.

There's people standing around waving cell phones, recording the murder scene—that kid's body will overflow on the Internet before the night is over. His body will pop up on his mother's Facebook, and all of her friends will see it. It will end up on Instagram and Twitter feeds, and people will watch, share, then repeat. The video of that kid's body will end up in homes that will never know the feeling of seeing that live.

He was just a kid.

Blood marinates his scalp, and his bulging eyeballs, and covers all of his gold teeth. His jaw is sliced in half, from the bullet. His shoes are divorced from his feet, from the impact of the bullet. His peeled skin is on the concrete, intimate with cigarette butts, Band-Aids, and rat shit—because of the bullet.

The kid is gone—he's not coming back. His parents will not raise the rest of their kids the same because that's what trauma does—sucks energy out of your performance. The children, his friends and loved ones, will not be the same. The people who witnessed the murder will not be the same. The kid is gone— a spiritual, emotional, mental, and future financial backbone is gone. Anyone who has proximity to this kid will not the same, and even if you don't say it aloud, you wonder, "Will I be next?"

I was a child when I first realized that nothing, or no one lasts forever. People leaving was routine. I remember walking home from school and seeing the entire inside, furnishings and possessions, of my friend's family's home on their front yard—landlords kicked them out for unpaid rent. I'd see my parents get handcuffed and escorted to jail in cop cars. Some friends would leave in body bags. Custody battles between two parents on the street always ended up with some kind of physical violence—heartbreak is why they left. In my neighborhood leaving was normal, and it was always abrupt. It was never like in the movies. No one wrote any notes and explained to people why they left. It wasn't like the workplace, there was no two weeks' notice. The adults in my life that held authority positions, like teachers and family, were gifted at making children believe they knew everything about the world until it was time to discuss departure. No one had the knowledge, or the guts, to explain why people left, or if they'd ever return.

"Why do so many people get killed in the summertime?" I asked my grandmother as a child. She answered me as clear as she could: It was because the summertime heat "goes to people's heads," which makes them act out of character, or because the children aren't in school, so now they have more time to "get in trouble," or because people just like to "show off." She concluded her monologues with "that's just what happens in the summertime . . . a lot of niggas die."

Summers in Baltimore are an old pair of tennis shoes—my parents walked them, I walked them, and the tennis shoes are currently on the feet of the youth. Under normal circumstances, if you ride through pretty much any neighborhood in East Baltimore, you'll see packs of kids outside cracking open fire hydrants, eating chicken boxes standing on corners, scraping frozen sugar out of Styrofoam cups with spoons, and watching the 12 O'Clock Boys perform death-threading stunts up and down the block. The old heads were always out there too, playing spades on fold-up tables, cans of Bud Ice, yelling about who's the greatest NBA Hall of Famer—it's always a party. It's common for parties to get broken up. I mean, was the party really that poppin' if it wasn't on the verge of getting broken up and shut down? Maybe it was because of a fistfight, or a neighbor making complaints, which prompted the cops to come and close the party down. Whether it was during grade school, high school, or as an undergrad everyone has attended a function that was broken up.

When a party gets broken up by bullets, it's different. Shots ring off and everyone's ducking, screaming, running, or all three. The second the smoke clears, you look around and realize no one was shooting at you or the people you were chilling with—the gun roar was echoing from around the corner. So everyone who has legs runs toward the sound of the fire, because the gun told us to—the gun is the puppeteer. While running, I'm pretty sure the same thought is on the forefront of everyone's mind: the body will belong to one of us. No matter how fast you run to the scene, the majority of the time the police will beat you there because there are one too many in our neighborhood, and they stay on the prowl.

The summer is over, and the K-12 school year starts and there will be Black boys and girls sitting in steaming hot classrooms with no AC, reading from ancient textbooks, and on the receiving end of being miseducated; and their creativity, critical and analytic thinking will be threatened because of this miseducation and of not being represented in the literature being taught.

It eventually goes from hot to cold, and soon it's the Christmas season—but the lack of heat causes devastation. Bills go unpaid, and families use their ovens to heat up their homes, and use candles for light, which end up burning down homes and taking away lives. In these houses, kids eat paint chips and are severely affected by lead paint poisoning, and through it all, we have to walk the streets and keep our head on the swivel because Baltimore police have a long track record of robbing, planting drugs and guns, and murdering innocent people. All of this pain comes with my Black experience in Baltimore.

Toni Morrison said, "History is percentiles, the thoughts of great men, and the description of eras." Eras of racism constantly change. Our ancestors' era was rife with lynchings, cotton, and Black human beings sold for crates of gun powder and rum—that's how it was taught to me.

We live in an era now where we can open an app on our phone, read a bible scripture, swipe to another app, and see a video of the White killer cop Derek Chauvin kneeling on George Floyd's neck while he was handcuffed and lying on his stomach for eight minutes, crying for his dead mother, until the he himself was dead—murdered.

In 1901, Theodore Roosevelt wrote to his friend Owen Wister, an American writer and historian: "I entirely agree with you that as a race and in the mass [Blacks] are altogether inferior to Whites. I suppose I should be ashamed to say that I take the Western View of the Indian. I don't go so far as to think that the only good Indians are the dead Indians, but I believe nine out of every ten are, and I shouldn't like to inquire too closely into the case of the tenth. The most vicious cowboy has more moral principal than the average Indian."

Roosevelt's quote encompasses why the police in Shelby, North Carolina, could buy the twenty-one-year-old White supremacist Dylan Roof Burger King, because "he hadn't eaten in a couple of days." This was hours after his arrests for killing nine Black churchgoers. And after, they can label him "very quiet, very calm," and note that "he was not problematic." Dylan Roof was an agent of the state, carrying out his ancestor's plans, which is to eliminate Black life.

In 1751, Benjamin Franklin wrote the essay "Observations Concerning the Increase of Mankind, Peopling of Countries, etc.," where he stated, "Why increase the sons of Africa, by planting them in America, where we have so fair an opportunity, by excluding all Blacks and Tawneys, of increasing the lovely white and red?" Franklin made it clear that he did not want Black people in this country, but since we were here, how would we preserve and increase the White population? You create laws and policies that discriminate against the descendants of Africa—Black people—to do so. You use propaganda to install racist ideas to the masses that will force Black people into prison cells, and keep White people out. You have racist policies that will ensure inferior opportunities and circumstances, so you can blame them and not the system that oppresses them. Then you condition them to believe the "up by the bootstraps" ideology, so they will blame themselves for not having, and not being afforded, the same opportunities that White people have in this country.

I didn't know what systemic oppression was, and that the pain I suffered from was a product of my era of racism, until I was an adult.

I didn't believe that mass incarceration was a real thing. Although I knew people, including myself, who were arrested and jailed for crimes we didn't commit, it was difficult for me to understand that millions of Blacks got arrested because of an "agenda." I knew that the county and private schools were better than the city schools but did not know that this was my era of racism. I just always thought that there was something wrong with Black people.

The pain that I endured, without any truthful context as to why that pain exists, is what forms and nourishes racist ideas to exist. If I see someone get shot, then see someone else get shot, the smart thing for me to do is to get a gun. Now I'm staying dangerous—staying on the alert. Then say I got arrested with that gun, people from all sides will call me a thug and a no-good knucklehead, when in all actuality, I'm trying to protect myself and my grandmother because the dudes across the street got shot. I might go to an HBCU and not know what the acromyn stands for, because I've never seen anybody go to one before, so an elite Black person might say I'm an idiot, when in actuality, I haven't been exposed to it, or never seen it on television. Or add to the fact that some of our parents didn't even graduate high school, so how could they ever teach us what an HBCU (Historically Black Colleges and Universities) is, and the importance of it. These stereotypes I face, and things I go through, add to the racist ideas than anyone and everyone can consume and produce. Why do they exist? My Black American experience can detail that.

Both White and Black people who have no proximity to poor people in communities like mine, and what we go through, frequently ask questions in regard to understanding racial injustices in this country that are not a part of their reality. I realized that it's about getting them to understand that it is indeed a part of their reality, and our two different worlds are merely two sides of the same coin.

Baltimore operates the way it does because people made conscious decisions to fund highways for White people in the suburbs, instead of jobs and education in the city for Black students. Baltimore operates the way it does because conscious decisions were made to pay out millions of dollars in lawsuits because police can't stop terrorizing the people they are supposed to protect and serve. A conscious decision was made to fund the police department and prisons, and not to build up undeserved Black communities. There are both White and Black

Americans who support the construction of more prisons, and they champion the strategy to add more police on the streets because there's a fixed image in their minds of poor Black people—they are inherently criminal—and the eradication of crime will protect their lives and valuables in their suburban homes.

Studies show that more police and more prisons do not lower the crime rate, but jobs and opportunities do. The decisions that benefit White suburbia are the same decisions that make the lives of Black residents in Baltimore City difficult. These decisions played a part in creating the conditions of my life story that I speak about. I've had several White people tell me that they can count how many times they've seen police in their neighborhoods, which is a luxury, being that people in my community see the police 24/7. In White suburbia, their schools and youth programs are funded, instead of policed. The adults in these suburban communities have the luxury to swoop in and support their kids who misbehave instead of them being punished by the legal system. Their kids' futures are protected, rather than encumbered with criminal records, even if they are arrested.

I still hang in the community where I come from, talk to my childhood friends regularly, and before the pandemic, I spent a large portion of my time in majority Black and inner-city schools. Whether it's graduate school, giving speeches, or in the literary world, I find myself in spaces with White and Black people who are not aware of my social context, or my upbringing. Through my storytelling, people find themselves having a better understanding of poor race relations in this country, how they contribute to the issues of racism and inequality, and ways that they can help combat these critical matters and become antiracist.

When thinking about "how to start the conversation about

race," dive into your own story, and your life. Be honest about how you have participated in racism. If you've lived in America, you have, there's no way that you haven't. But maybe you don't realize you have? Be honest about your ignorance and ask questions. Be honest about your experiences. Just how I didn't realize that racism was a part of my reality, the people who are furthest away might not see it.

My experiences of being Black and from Baltimore have been buried under politics, polls, and mainstream media. Not only have I survived violent murders, police brutality, and poverty, I've been trying to dive deep and examine my experiences, analyze my suffering, and develop liberatory ideas to help me grow, and share truth through my poetry, storytelling, essays and spoken word, what I hope can be useful to others.

In this book, I will explore ways to combat racist ideas through understanding the complexities of various Black experiences. With these thoughts, essays, analyses, and experiences of what it's like growing up in the Baltimore I know so well, my objective is to provide in these chapters the basis of understanding from which conversations can be held and action can be taken. I chose to combat racism through this lens so that people don't have to face the same roadblocks early on, and thus, become antiracist earlier on. The same way I put my story out is the same way I have to understand someone else's story and unlearn the falsehoods I was conditioned to believe about them. Doing the antiracist work is acknowledging someone else's story, someone else's pain—and not discounting their journey. However, don't confuse just knowing someone's story and reading about antiracism work with actually doing the work to become antiracist. Both need to exist.

James Baldwin once said, "Soldiers don't, statesmen don't, pastors don't, union leaders don't. Only the poets." As a poet, it's against my moral obligation to promote conformity, unlike the workers Baldwin mentioned above. Since I'm conscious of what's going on in this country when it comes to race relations, it's my duty to share my experiences. It is my duty to use my language to create spaces for people to grow in their antiracism work. Once you realize that something is going on and it needs to be fixed, it's up to you to create spaces for people to be vulnerable, to be honest, and to even show ignorance—and from this space, realization and growth occur.

All of these individuals and organizations currently mobilizing throughout the country are Black seeds being planted. Can these seeds bloom bright enough and stand strong enough to change race relations in an entire country? You have to understand that you do have power, and that you are a force of change. You, we, are all in positions to harness the energy for positive change and shift it to where it needs to go.

Writing and telling my story helped me learn to grow stronger in my antiracism work—something that we should all be doing. I'm not here to police or gain authority over Black liberation, but I am here to make people aware of the injustices that are rarely covered or encountered in-depth by mainstream media, whose spokespeople have little direct knowledge of the real issues, providing only quick statistics and surface analysis, and hardly ever giving platform to people who truly know the issues—from their root causes to workable solutions. It's past time to work together to give insight on how we all can do better.

The most important thing that I learned on my journey is that there is nothing wrong with Black people, and there is nothing extraordinary about White People. Black people are not inferior, but their opportunities in this country are. White people are not superior, but their opportunities in this country are.

One of the people who made me become stronger in my

antiracist work has been Dr. Ibram X. Kendi, author of *Stamped from the Beginning*, where he says, "Any effective solution of eradicating American racism must involve Americans committed to antiracist policies seizing and maintaining power over institutions, neighborhoods, counties, states, nations—the world. . . . An antiracist American can only be guaranteed if principled antiracists are in power, and then antiracist policies become the law of the land, and then antiracist ideas become the common sense of the people, and then the antiracist common sense of the people holds those antiracist leaders and policies accountable."[1]

Through my own experiences and research, I came to an understanding that growth and becoming antiracist are not a one-stop shop or a fixed state to be satisfied with, but a lifelong commitment to reexamining the way one thinks and the way one acts.

I do believe that we can live in a humane society one day. I believe that there will come a time when mothers and fathers won't have to bury their kids because they are victims of poverty. I believe we can one day live in a world without police. I believe that one day we can truly live in an antiracist society. Being on the journey to become antiracist is a freedom that I never knew existed. A freedom that is available to us all. A freedom that belongs to us all.

---

1   Kendi, Ibram X. *Stamped from the Beginning*, Bold Type Books (New York 2016), 510.

The Art of Robbin' and Stealin'

Me and my homies had to be around eleven or twelve years old. Doing what we do best when we weren't at school—hanging on an East Baltimore corner in our neighborhood with one another. Mikey, Adrian, John-John, Tori, and myself were the only ones out this day. Mikey has been my boy since we were kids, when we found out that our mothers were best friends. Mikey's skin complexion is jet black, and his body is all lips, legs, and arms—his torso is infant-shoe short.

"Mannnn, I'm mad as hell right now," Mikey said while hitting a blunt.

"Why?" I looked up at him, while spitting sunflower seed shells to the pavement.

"Cause yo, my mother talkin' about she don't got no money so I can go to the freak party on Easter."

Not sure what other cultures call their first preteen parties that involve twerking, but in Baltimore, we call 'em freak parties. These types of parties are our rights of passage into big boy/big girl world. If you ask anyone from my city, I'm sure they'll remember their first freak party, or their early freak party days. They'll be able to detail the music that was playing, to the outfit from head to toe, to the first person they shared their "real" dance with.

I remember my first one, like it was last night. This was back when Carmelo Anthony was playing for the Denver Nuggets, and the Nike Huaraches 2K4s had just come out. I was amongst the few who had a pair, because I got them as soon as they released. My outfit wasn't complete until the lady Shawn came to my crib and got me all set. Shawn was a booster, her full-time job was stealing clothes from malls, and selling to people in our neighborhood at discounted prices. She'd knock on our front door with a large trash bag filled with her stolen goods. Even if I wasn't looking for any new clothes, whenever Shawn came around, my grandmother would buy from her because she had those deals that no one should turn down. My grandmother bought me some blue jeans that were triple my size, because that's how we dressed back then, and my freak party outfit was complete, and I was set.

Mikey went on a twenty-minute rant about how he didn't have the money to attend the party, and we told him that we'd scrape up money for both his outfit and the entry fee. Mikey then stopped midconversation and pulled a black metal BB gun out of his bag. To the naked eye it looked real, but if you got close enough you could tell that he painted the orange tip on the front of the gun with a black sharpie to make it look authentic.

"What you pulling that out for? What, you tryna shoot some rats? If not, I can get the real pistol," John-John said.

"Nah, I wanna hit a lick. Them muhfuckas that live in Canton is rich. If I don't get too close to 'em, they won't know it's a BB gun."

Canton is a neighborhood that's a mile away from my East Baltimore home where I grew up. Canton is filled with popular sports bars, seafood restaurants, and other fine dining eateries that sit on the historic waterfront. Statistical Atlas[1] reports that the median household income in Canton is $100,900, and its employment rate is 80 percent. And my neighborhood, McElderry Park, which we call "Down Da Hill," has a median household income of $35,700, and an employment rate of 53.9 percent. Me and my friends didn't know much about percentages, let alone the difference in median incomes around the city, but we could eyeball the wealth gap between Down Da Hill and Canton.

Me and my homies' middle schools were either located in Canton, or nearby, so we were in that neighborhood often. We drooled over the huge homes and imagined they had ice machines on their refrigerators, a luxury that none of us had, the latest model foreign cars that we pictured ourselves in the driver seat of, fancy private swimming pools, exclusive thousand-dollar pedal bikes, the cleanliness and quietness of their neighborhoods—it was paradise so close, but yet so far.

Me and my homies stuck together, even if we didn't 100 percent want to, because we loved one another. If one of the homies wanted to hit a lick, no matter if it was to get money for pampers, food, clothes, or to help their parents out with bills—we rode for each other. My homies would always hail me as the "smart one," in the group, so when it came to planning the licks, I'd be the quarterback. I premeditated the times we walked into bakeries and ran out with the tip jar, splitting it down the middle between us. I scoped out people's backyards where they kept those thousand-dollar bikes and devised plans on how to acquire them—it didn't matter how secured their gates were, if

---

1   https://statisticalatlas.com/neighborhood/Maryland/Baltimore/Canton /Overview.

they were padlocked, we always found a way. I kept my head on the swivel for nice cars that we could target. Devising these robberies were my specialty, however, we didn't go through with all of them. Sometimes we got active, and other times, we didn't. It just felt good going deep into your imagination, envisioning a paradise that you might never experience. Whenever I talked about schemes, my homies' mouths sealed, and ears opened.

This particular day I told them that we don't need the BB gun, but we can keep it on deck, just in case. I knew about this White BMW a few blocks away on South Linwood Avenue that would be an easy finesse. After scoping the owner out for weeks, I peeped her morning routine. I noticed that she comes out of the house to start her car up, then goes back inside. But, when she goes in, it's either for roughly thirty seconds, when she's grabbing her house key, or purse, or some item that I'm assuming she forgot to bring out the first time. Or, she takes ten minutes and always comes out with a cup of coffee and a small child she straps in a car seat. So, if we go, we have to be careful when monitoring her timing after going inside of the house. When she goes back in the house after starting the car, we'll wait just thirty seconds, and if she doesn't come out, I'll rush to the driver side, hop in the car, and Mikey will hop in the passenger. If she or someone else comes out of the house while we're in motion, Mikey will aim the BB gun at them, and threaten them with a meeting with the man upstairs, which will make any sane person relax. Once we pull off in the car, we'll head back down to the block and pick up John-John, Adrian, and Tori. Then, we can go on Monument Street and purchase some CDs so we can have some real music to listen to. After that, we can go cop some grass, some liquor, then head down on Clinton Street to hang out with Brianna and her homegirls for the evening. After that, I know this house that we can hit, and take whatever we want—it's up there near Morgan State University. One of my cousins lives on that block, and he said there's this dude who works the night shift and always leaves his front door unlocked when he goes out. We can go inside, grab any valuables we see, then roll out—it'll be easy and quick. After, we drive back toward the block, drop off the goods that we stole at the vacant house on the block, and then find somewhere to ditch the car. Then, we can all go home and figure out what's on the agenda for tomorrow. That was my plan.

As youngins, me and my friends were ignorant to local politics; however, it didn't take rocket science to see that there wasn't a political party to represent our interests. Still, my friends and I were repeatedly told by adults that our living situations would not improve, and we'd never receive what we'd need in life, unless young Black people like ourselves voted when we became of age. The men and women that I saw running for office on television were not blasting Boosie or Lil' Kim or Jay Z or Lil Wayne during their campaign trails. None of these politicians and candidates spoke in the same vernacular as my friends and me. I didn't see any guys with suits and ties ordering from the same carry-outs we ate from. If they did come to our neighborhoods, it was for photo ops and to gain media attention to create a false perception that they cared about us. None of these people in positions of power were reflections of my friends and me. So we didn't rally behind officials, but instead, behind one another. We roamed the streets that conceived us and took ownership of public spaces, stole valuable items from those who have plenty. We created our own laws and delegated representatives in our neighborhood who we saw fit. There wasn't any love for kids like us on the big screen or in the newspapers, or in the books, so we found love and loyalty in one another. Growing up, everyone wanted to speak for us. Not

to us. Not with us. But about us. And we never were offered a
seat at the table.

Our language was always silenced, unless it was used on a
basis to show that we're "ignorant" and "don't talk right." And
when we did try to speak on what we wanted, what we deserved,
and what we needed, we got shut down and were told to "stay in
a child's place." We were always the topic of discussion when it
was about violence, or welfare, or criminality, or low test scores.
This was our experience growing up, and it is still commonplace for the younger generation of Black children growing up
in Baltimore City.

*How many times did we tell you, America, that we were hun-
gry? How many times did we tell you we were hungry for love?
How many times did we tell you we were hungry for a way out?
How many times did we tell you we were hungry for something as
simple as a fair chance? How many times did we show you we were
hungry for the truth?*

Bessie Smith warned us in her song "Jail-House Blues,"
when she sang, "Lord, this house is gonna get raided." In an on-
camera interview, 2Pac revealed to us what that raid would look
like. He told us a story about some folks inside of a hotel room
who have "plenty" of food, and who denied entry to a hungry
and poor group of friends who needed to eat. Those inside the
hotel opened the door, and the hungry folks were able to see
inside—there was a party, practically throwing around an abun-
dance of food; however, they tell the group of friends there's no
food there. Every day, this group tries to sing their way into the
hotel room, "we are hungry please let us in." A week later the
song becomes more demanding, "we hungry, we need some
food!" After three weeks the bass in the voice grows thick and
angry, "get me some food or we breaking down the door!"

The group of friends went back to the drawing board and

realized they had to adopt a new language if they wanted to eat. Out of the many languages they could've chosen from, they chose the one that's closes to them, an American manifesto—gun talk. There was no future in asking, so "picking the lock, coming through blasting," is what they did, 2Pac said. That group of friends traded in their "Kumbaya, my Lord" for Biggie's "Gimmie the Loot," which became the soundtrack for these artful dodgers. When it's time to eat a meal, they rob and steal to silence their rumbling tummies. They smash and grab, turning their hangout spots into Aladdin's cave.

Let me ask you this, why would the children suck blood out of a stone, when the gun that America gave them is eye-glued to a body? America loses its mind when its loved ones are chewed up but never showed the children how to fish properly. The children see that there is a paradise, and it's nearby, and that they can't come in. They see no future in asking, and there's no future in the word "wait," which they are always told, while being handed crumbs, if "lucky." Somehow, everyone is appalled when the children chew off their tongues and use bullets for rebuttals. Y'all wonder why the murder rate in Baltimore has been giraffe neck since the seventies? The way children react to bondage is the truth hunting us down. The truth that we neglect. So now the children bring violence to the party—they come just to fuck it up and leave. The children show us what happens when you boot-heel a people, instead of nurturing them and giving them the best that you have to offer. Giving them the necessities that you promise them, but never deliver.

Education behind the Bars
of Poverty

M y mother got pregnant with me in '92, and because of her cocaine and heroin addiction, my grandmother decided to quit her job working at Signet Bank, turning down a promotion, so she could pursue a career in daycare, to provide for me, my mother's unborn child. During my early childhood, my grandmother made financial sacrifices to enroll me in Catholic school because she believed that those institutions had better teachers, and she assumed that these institutions valued the students more than public schools did. Both my mother and father dropped out of high school, so my grandmother made it her duty to ensure that I wouldn't end up like my parents.

Aside from attending the Salvation Army's Early Head Start Program as a toddler, the first school I attended was St. Elizabeth, a few blocks from my house, a stone's throw from Patterson Park. After I completed third grade, St. Elizabeth got shut down—from what I remember hearing, financial issues—then merged with Our Lady of Pompei—a school undergoing the same issues— which then turned into Archbishop Borders. Archbishop Borders was on Conkling Street in the Highlandtown area. I knew that it cost my grandmother cash to put me through school, but I never asked how much. I do know that her paying tuition swapped out name brand cereal and other household luxuries.

Archbishop Borders's classes were extremely small, and it was majority Black and Hispanic, and there were sprinkles of White students. Our uniform consisted of shirts and ties, and girls wore skirts. From pre-K till about fourth grade I received straight A's and perfect attendance. My family and friends were under the assumption that I was in love with education; however, that was not true. The real reason I used to get straight A's is because my Aunt Sadiq used to give me $20 for every A I received on my report card. Therefore, I was in it for the money, not for learning purposes. This became evident that it was the case because around the time I hit middle school, my aunt stopped giving me money, and that's when the straight A's started to fade away. After my aunt stopped funding my good grades, I still stayed afloat in the classroom—my performance was decent. I don't remember too much of the nature of how my teachers taught me, or what they taught. I'd only be able to remember the names of the basic courses like social studies, language arts, religion, math, etc. I do remember all of my teachers being older White women. I remember that my first and last time having a Black teacher was in the seventh grade. His name was Mr. Gibson, and he always reminded us that he wasn't just a "regular Black guy," he was half Filipino.

I wouldn't call myself a class clown, but, in elementary and middle school, I had the power to make my classmates laugh at will, which prompted several phone calls home to my grandmother, and teacher conferences about my behavior. Whenever I acted up in school, my grandmother threatened me with sending me to public school. What my grandmother didn't realize at the time is that her telling me this amplified my bad behavior because I knew that public schools were much funner than my school, and I'd get a chance to be around my friends. There was a middle school around the corner from Archbishop Borders called Highlandtown Middle, and damn near everyone from my neighborhood attended there. I got out of school an hour before my friends at Highlandtown, so as soon as the bell rang, I snatched off my tie, took off my button-up shirt, and had my friends sneak me in the back door of their school.

Highlandtown was pure anarchy, to say the least. The hallways were filled with kids dumping blunt guts on the floors and drinking alcohol. You'd see couples making out, dice games erupting on every floor, fistfights that sometimes even involved students and teachers. The students regularly set fires in the bathrooms so the school could get shut down for the day. If you were in class, it wasn't strange to see students toss textbooks out of the window mumbling, "I hate this fuckin' work." Highlandtown seemed like the perfect fit for me at the time.

I hated following rules, so my grandmother didn't know that she was threatening me with a good time by saying that she'd send me to Highlandtown. It never happened, I graduated from Archbishop Borders, attended Archbishop Curley High School freshman year, then transferred to Baltimore City College High School. City was considered one of the "good" schools. Personally, it didn't reflect what everyone made it cracked up to be. We had outdated textbooks, we completed work at old desks, but it was still "better" than the other schools, people would say. I skipped class a lot, sold weed and snacks to the student body, spent many of my hours running the hallways or in the locker room shooting craps, or spending time with my girlfriend, Ameesha. Intellectually, I believed that Ameesha was light-years ahead of me, and if I was basing it off classroom performance, her grades reflected that, too.

She was ranked in the top half of the class, turned in all of her work on time, rarely missed school, and was just an all-around scholar. I was the complete opposite. I wasn't ranked in the top of the class, turned in my work late; and no one ever called me scholar or praised me for my classroom performances. I had more faith in Ameesha's future than I did in my own. Outside of her aspirations she exposed me to a lifestyle that was outside of the parameters of my day-to-day life, such as going on my first diner date experience at Fridays in Towson, MD. She had dreams of becoming a nurse, and I remember telling her that I didn't know what my future looked like, aside from making enough money to survive. I ended up skating by, all the way to high school graduation, which was a milestone for me and my family.

When I became an adult, I saw the real underlying issues of how and why schools like Highlandtown existed in a rich state like Maryland, and it all made sense.

The state of Maryland simply robs Baltimore students of their education, and it's always on the forefront of the media for the world to see. From the TV show *The Wire*, which brought attention to Baltimore's drug epidemic, corrupt politics, crooked cops, gun violence, and poverty—to constantly being in the media for our yearly high murder rates. Whenever the topic of Baltimore politics gets brought up, I immediately turn the conversation to the city schools and the students. I tell people to visit the city's majority Black schools, then visit the county and majority White schools, and see for themselves.

If you can't physically make it to the classroom, the film *Hard Times at Douglass High: A No Child Left Behind Report Card* that was aired on HBO in 2008 (directed by Alan Raymond and Susan Raymond) showcases some of the issues in our city schools. It was centered around the 2005 school year at Frederick Douglass High School in Baltimore and the injustices and harsh realities of what many students faced—and still face today. The school was on the verge of being sanctioned if they did not improve their test scores by 2007. They were struggling to meet President Bush's No Child Left Behind Act of 2002, a law that was created to provide equal educational opportunities for students in poverty, those who receive special education services, and those with other disadvantages. The film has some uplifting moments; however, the struggles overpowered the film. The film encapsulated everything from a young English teacher quitting in the middle of the year, fist-fights in the hallways, kids scrambling the hallways when they were supposed to be in class, and how the school frequently was being run with substitutes and other emergency fill-ins.

In recent years, Baltimore has yet again been in the media for its inadequate school systems. In early 2018, Baltimore was trending in the media due to the icebox conditions in some of the public schools—some thermostats read around 30 degrees.

Pictures of injustice made a lightning attack across the Internet—snapshots of Baltimore students wearing gloves, coats, and hats, and of the damage caused by broken boilers and bursting pipes. A similar story emerged in September of 2017, when classrooms inside of Patterson High School reached over 100 degrees for consecutive days, where students sweat bullets as they attempted to learn while being smothered in Satan's arms. The system's chief operations officer Keith Scroggins said, "We are doing everything we can to install air conditioning in our schools to make them more comfortable." And with "limited funding, the process is expected to take five years."[1]

---

1   Richman, Talia. "Baltimore classrooms top 100 degrees: 'It was impossible to learn.'" *Baltimore Sun*, September 26, 2017, https://www.baltimoresun .com/maryland/baltimore-city/bs-md-heat-patterson-high-school -20170926-story.html.

Baltimore is the largest city in the richest state in the US, and our children are forced to sit in these horrific conditions in places disguised as schools, and the excuse is "limited funding."

This might be someone's first time hearing about students being forced to flirt with death inside of public schools; however, America has maintained racial inequalities in education for many years.

On April 12, 1860, the Mississippi senator who later became president of the Confederacy, Jefferson Davis, delivered a speech objecting to a bill funding education in Washington DC. In his speech he stated, "This government was not founded by negroes nor for negroes but by White men for White men . . . the inequality of the White and Black races was 'stamped from the beginning.'" Davis and many other racists in this country have and still currently believe that Black people are biologically distinct from and inferior to White people. Therefore, handing something over as powerful as education to a group of subhuman Black monsters would be blasphemous, and it would debunk their beloved White supremacy.

November 1, 1864, was Maryland's Emancipation Day. In the book *Stamped from the Beginning,* Dr. Ibram X. Kendi wrote that the newly free people flashed and paraded to the president's house, where Lincoln gave a speech and encouraged them to improve their moral character and intellectual capacity. Lincoln said this but supported Maryland's constitution, which didn't allow Blacks to vote or attend public schools. Lincoln expected newly free Blacks to two-step into freedom without a stumble after being desecrated by slavery. That is the same ideology that people have when they expect students in Baltimore public schools to receive a quality education in heinous environments—only to blame the children, and not the school system that enslaves, oppresses, and miseducates Black children and the children of color.

I've spoke at several schools in Maryland, from suburban to urban, from majority Black to majority White schools. The suburban and majority White schools have floors clean enough to eat off of and are equipped with state-of-the-art technology. When I'm in the urban and majority Black schools I can't decipher whether the schools look like prisons, or the prisons look like these schools. The students read from ancient textbooks with missing pages, sit at the same desk that our great-grandparents sat at, and are being taught on hundred-year-old chalkboards.

In early 2017, the *Baltimore Sun* released an article that stated, "In the seven years since the first of Maryland's six casinos opened, they have pumped $1.7 billion into the state's Education Trust Fund."[2] The audacious claim that the state has "limited funding" is an insult to the people of Baltimore. Using the term "limited funding" is an escape to avoid providing a legitimate educational environment for Baltimore City students, forcing them to suffer in cruel conditions. Being as though it is politically incorrect for racists to use the "N-word" and call us biologically inferior, they swap it out with terms that drip with racism, such as "limited funding."

When talking about "low test scores" or "disruptive Black students," the basic resources that these children lack always gets left out of the narrative. The State of Maryland opened a $35 million youth detention facility in Baltimore, but officials say that it'll take up to five years for the city schools to have something as basic as air and heat. This sends a message to the entire Black community—the US government is more focused

---

2   Broadwater, Luke, and Green, Erica L. "Maryland casinos are pumping out billions for education. So why are there school budget deficits?" *Baltimore Sun*, January 22, 2017, https://www.baltimoresun.com/maryland/bs-md -casino-education-20170121-story.html.

on padlocking Black youths in prison cells, as opposed to giving them valuable education. We don't need anyone to say, "America doesn't care about black people," when actions—or lack thereof—speak volumes. In the middle of the COVID-19 pandemic, Maryland's Governor Larry Hogan proposed a cut of $345 million from public schools. A racist decision that will further widen the inequity gap between wealthier county schools and underfunded city schools, creating more disparities.

Sister Souljah once said, "the sincerity of all of the programs and all of the education has to be questioned, indicted, convicted, because the bottom line is that America is not and has never tried to produce African adults who are functional, self-sufficient, who understand their politics, their economics, and their relationship to the world politics and world economics."

Given the context of how Baltimore City schools are operated, you can see why many Black students are apprehensive about attending school, strictly from the nature of their environment.

On top of this, students are being forced to learn and engage with literature that does not reflect who they are—and it's the reason why I thought that I hated reading growing up.

The bulk of children's literature is unfairly White. The Cooperative Children's Book Center at the University of Wisconsin shows us that "In 2016, 427 books were written or illustrated by people of color, and 736 books about people of color, out of the 3,400 books it analyzed—which adds up to 22 percent of children's books."[3]

---

3   Donnella, Leah. "People of Color Accounted for 22 Percent of Children's Books Characters in 2016." NPR.org, February 17, 2017, https://www .npr.org/sections/codeswitch/2017/02/17/515792141/authors-and -illustrators-of-color-accounted-for-22-percent-of-children-s-books#:~:text =On%20Wednesday%2C%20the%20Cooperative%20Children's,22%20 percent%20of%20children's%20books.

This is literary racism, and it negatively impacts all students in various ways. It creates a literacy disconnect for Black students and other students of color that excludes their life experiences, and an actual engagement divide between these students and White students. Because of the lack of representation in the classroom, we are conditioned to believe that our stories, experiences, cultures, and dialects are seen as having little or no value in academic settings, which can sometimes trickle into everyday lives. Studies show that students are the least engaged in literature when they don't see themselves in it. These students then are judged by their "lack" of performance in the classroom, which is ultimately caused by racial biases.

The racial biases in the work that is taught doesn't only hinder the Black students and the students of color, but it impacts the White students, too. Due to White students not engaging in literature written by and about Black people, they are conditioned to feel superior among non-White students. It also prevents White children from developing the humility necessary to cooperate with people who are not of European ancestry. This is one of the many ways this country fuels White supremacy, and it starts within the classroom.

Knowingly or unknowingly, White teachers in these classrooms have always had gifted Black students all around them; however, the White teacher will bond with the White student, ignoring the intellect of the Black child. They bond with the White student because they see them as a part of themselves. They don't see the Black child as a gift, but a threat to their existence. How do White teachers negotiate that? If they are conscious of this iniquity, they will nurture the Black child to that child's full potential, even if the Black child surpasses the White Child. Or, they display cognitive dissonance to either minimize the Black child, or destroy him, and more often than not, they destroy.

White people need to be truly knowledgeable about the fallacies of their own existence. When they don't know about Black history, this further aids and abets the notion of White privilege. We are not taught the truth about who we are, because to teach us, and them, about who we are is to destroy White supremacy and White privilege.

What do we do as educators? We have to realize that there is no middle ground when it comes to the needs of our Black students and students of color. As educators, if we do not ensure that every member in the classroom is valued and well represented through the work that we teach, then we stand behind the line of literary racism, whether we want to accept the truth or not. For non-White and White educators, when it comes to assigning books to read in the classroom, if you find yourself having trouble with keeping your students engaged, feel free to reach out to experts who can guide you in the right direction. We must give our children a large view of the Black/POC (People of Color) experience, and that can be done by having more diverse books, and by finding creative ways for children to tell their own stories, and not have someone else tell it for them.

For a long time in this country, Black people and people of color never had the luxury to tell their own stories, therefore, educators need to listen to their students when they advise them on what they need in order to become self-sufficient in this society. The White people who were always efficient in literature, journalism, and art told the world fallacies about how we feel, what we love, what we hate, what we like to do, etc. Now that we have the platforms to tell our own stories, it's important that we do—which will not only give honest accounts of who we are and what's going on on our side, but it will motivate others to share their stories, as well.

When I look back at what I was taught in school, my Black

experience was omitted entirely, or it was scarcely mentioned. There weren't any Black characters who walked, talked, dressed, and shared similar thoughts as I.

We need to approach and teach literacy in a way that shows students it's more than just an "in the classroom," term that revolves around passing monologues and receiving grades on tests and quizzes. Literacy is the conduit where people gain access into a world where they can engage, analyze, and critique their own thoughts and actions; and is also an entrance into another's space and universe. Understanding the importance of literacy will improve students' performance in the classroom, and critical thinking skills that will grant students the mental bandwidth to make more sophisticated decisions in life, and to solve problems when they must face them. As educators and parents, we have to teach literacy as a tool of intelligence that will equip our students to maneuver through the world that stretches way beyond the walls of the classroom, and I believe that many students will then have a different outlook on the benefits of literacy.

Students will engage more in literacy when they see themselves in the literature they are being taught. The world's hegemonic understanding of literacy today is an outmoded and racist paradigm that stifles the progression of Black children and children of color inside and outside of the classroom. We have to prove to the students that we value every member of the classroom by providing them with texts and other forms of art that are parallel to their social context.

Relatability through literacy will crack the shell of racism in the classroom, eliminating the opportunity gap. We will not develop a system that is truly antiracist if we do not change the way that literacy is taught in our schools. Black students and students of color stories matter, and we need to add meaning to our students' lives, using the classroom.

For too many moons, America has been lying to Black children. In order to aid in righting these wrongs, every teacher who works with Black students needs to be honest with the students they are teaching. Day one of class, after the introductions and icebreakers, students need to be put on game to the laws and policies that are hindering them to learn how to deal with life as they must face it. Learning is revolution. Writing and teaching the truth is political and revolutionary. If we want to threaten White supremacy and its standing, then we need to teach students how to deal with life and how they must face it.

Many teachers are not responding to the students' needs because they approach teaching in a "y'all don't know anything . . . I'm here to teach you . . . I'm right, you're wrong" kind of attitude—instead of teaching in a manner that reflects the students.

The student-teacher relationship should be a relationship where both parties learn from each other. Teachers ride to work through neighborhoods where their students live and see the disconnect from their personal lives and the material they are trained to teach. Teachers are with these students five days a week; they read the personal essays about their lives; they hear the students converse among one another. They know that their favorite rappers are NBA YoungBoy and Megan Thee Stallion, which is literature rapped over beats, but they turn around and give them Shakespeare. Why? These teachers watch the news and read the paper—they know the state cares more about pushing students into prisons rather than toward promise. However, they still deny these students the opportunity to be free within the classroom. They deny them promise and possibility and instead aid in their punishment and imprisonment by not teaching them how to deal with the world and how they must face it.

I know for a fact that if the younger version of myself would have received books that valued and represented my experiences well, it wouldn't have taken me until I was a college student to realize the importance of literacy, and how it can impact my life in a positive way on various levels.

I mention outside of the classroom because there is a life outside of memorizing monologues and receiving good grades on tests and quizzes. Depending on what you read and what you don't read, and how your teachers teach, will shape your future, and the decisions you make, and the opportunities you take advantage of.

You, the students, must make sure that they show you that they value you, by reaching you in a way that will produce a functional and more self-sufficient version of you, who understand the importance of education, literacy, and your relationship to the world outside of the classroom. Not every instructor will deliver, so it's also mandatory that you seek knowledge on your own and indulge yourself in information that will teach you how to deal with the world and how you must face it.

No Love for the Landlords

A few summers ago, I was walking up Monument Street in 98-degree weather, shirtless, heading to North East Market, which is the only semifresh-food hub in my neighborhood. I ran into my childhood friend Chris, and he said, "Yo, I never knew you had that scar on your stomach. What happened?" I told him that I was diagnosed with Pyloric Stenosis as an infant and had to undergo a death-biting surgery to keep me alive, which left a permanent gash right above my belly button and another two on my right and lower abdomen. Chris's rebuttal was "That's crazy. I'm surprised you ain't die. You know Johns Hopkins be killing Black people." I didn't know what he meant, but that became a recurrent phrase that I heard then on out from people in my community. This made me recall the time my mother told me a story about how, after my surgery, the Johns Hopkins Hospital (JHH) workers declared me dead, which ended up being a "mistake," after they saw how berserk my mother went.

I wanted to find out more information regarding this alleged Black blood that JHH has had on its hands. I started to conduct some research and glued my eyes to texts, such as

Medical Apartheid by Harriet Washington; the JHH workers trying to kill me was no longer a mystery.

I read through the dark and disgusting studies of unethical medical experimentations on Black Americans from colo-
nial times to the present. I discovered that in the mid-1900s,
Baltimore's Kennedy Krieger Institute (KKI), an institute
affiliated with Johns Hopkins Hospital, held a "Lead-Based
Abatement and Repair and Maintenance Study." This study
kept or placed Black families who had small children in ram-
shackle homes, knowingly exposing them to dangerous levels of
lead. If lead paint were a basketball player, it would be a Hall of
Famer for causing severe illness and chronic mental retardation
in young children who inhale airborne lead dust and swallow the
paint chips like their favorite UTZ (snack food). KKI carried out
its agenda by working with landlords to lure Black families into
these lead-tainted homes with food stamps, money, toys, and
other necessities a poor family might need. This study was allegedly carried out to eliminate future lead threats. "They moni-
tored changes in the children's lead levels as well as the brain
and developmental damage that resulted from different kinds
of lead-abatement programs," according to *Medical Apartheid*. [1]
The parents were not informed that this study would be placing
children at a high risk of lead exposure.

After several years of taking advantage of and decimat-
ing thousands of Black children with lead paint poisoning, on
August 16, 2001, the courts ruled against this experiment, juxta-
posing it with the Tuskegee Syphilis Experiment. Judge J. Cathell
noted, "It can be argued that the researchers intended that the
children be the canaries in the mine."

When I originally read Judge J. Cathell's phrase, "canaries

---

1   Washington, Harriet A. *Medical Apartheid*, Doubleday (New York 2007).

in the mine," I didn't know what it meant, but a quick Google search changed that. In the 20th century, miners would tote canaries with them into the tunnels when working. If dangerous gasses, such as carbon monoxide, were in the tunnels, it would kill the innocent canaries before killing the miners, providing them with a clear-cut warning to immediately evacuate the tunnels or put on protective respirator gear.

I said to myself, "Damn, that's really messed up, canaries didn't deserve that." Canaries in the mine were guiltless creatures who were being murdered for research purposes, which was arguably to help build a better world. But some would say the sacrifice of canaries was in "God's plan," which doesn't make sense to me. But then again, the desire to oppress and murder the vulnerable has never been justified with logic here in America. The justification to oppress and murder has never been based on facts; instead, it is based on false beliefs.

Do you think that in God's little notepad, he wrote, "These canaries are meant to be captive, held against their will, and murdered"? Or, "After we release the shackles and chains from these Black folks, we're gonna create racist laws and policies to keep them padlocked to poverty, prison cells, and an unfair lifestyle while living in America"? Nah, I don't believe that.

Canaries were not born with the sole purpose of being prisoners of miners. The people in my community were not born with the sole purpose of being prisoners of the American streets that conceived them.

* * *

"Why White people don't live around here?" A question I remember asking my grandmother as a child. She laughed, then said, "They don't wanna live around here with us, and they don't want us living where they at. That's why all them on the other side of the park, and we on this side," pointing to Patterson Park, which was a few blocks away from us. She then told me how she moved on the block in which we were living in 1989, making her the second Black family. Other than the White man Mr. Skylark who lived next door to us for a couple of years until he died, my neighborhood was all Black. The only White people that we saw regularly were teachers, police officers, doctors, landlords, and there would be a few White heroin addicts lingering around. My grandmother's response to my "Why White people don't live around here?" was the best way she could explain housing segregation to me, which I never heard of before until I was well into my twenties. Growing up, racist ideas made me believe that White people live in neighborhoods with bigger homes, cleaner streets, and less police because they deserved more than us. But in reality, laws were created with the intent for them to have more than us.

Professor Emeritus of Law Garrett Power's "Apartheid Baltimore Style: The Residential Segregation Ordinances of 1910–1913" provides strong historical context that reveals serious problems in Baltimore. On December 17, 1910, City Solicitor Edgar Allan Poe voiced his opinion with regard to an ordinance that would keep Blacks and Whites segregated in Baltimore. Poe said, "because of irrefutable facts, well-known conditions, inherent personal characteristics, and ineradicable traits of character peculiar [sic] to the races, close association on a footing of absolute equality is utterly impossible between them, wherever Negroes exist in large numbers in a White community, and invariably leads to irritation, friction, disorder and strife."[2] The oppressors and beneficiaries of White supremacy will never call "the oppressed" by that name, because it will

---

2   Power, Garrett. "Apartheid Baltimore Style: the Residential Segregation Ordinances of 1910–1913." Md. L. Rev V. 289 (1983), https://digitalcom -mons.law.umaryland.edu/mlr/vol42/iss2/4.

then be an admission to the discrimination they are responsible for. So instead, they say things like Poe, "well-known conditions," which are the slums that were created by their ancestors. "Inherent personal characteristics and ineradicable traits of character" is another way to say born criminals and savages, but racists never speak about the savagery of the laws that keep Black people padlocked to poverty.

Power tell us that many progressives believed that poor Black people should be isolated in their own neighborhoods in order to maintain peace and reduce incidents of civil disturbance. These progressives also believed that such "isolation" was necessary in order to protect property values among the White majority, and to prevent the spread of communicable disease into the nearby White neighborhoods, but little did they see that their racist ideas were the real communicable disease that was spreading.

Less than a year after Edgar Allan Poe's racist and classist rhetoric, Baltimore Mayor J. Barry Mahool signed into law "a[n] ordinance for preserving peace, preventing conflict and ill feeling between white and colored races in Baltimore City, and promoting the general welfare of the city by providing, so far as practicable, for the use of separate blocks by White and colored people for residences, churches and schools."[3] This was the first housing segregation law in the United States of this caliber aimed toward Black people. Mahool was also hailed as an "earnest advocate" for "good government" and stood up for women's suffrage and social justice. Pretty sure he and others would label himself as "not racist," although we can see he clearly was, from the laws he signed that discriminated against Black people. This law set the stage for inequality throughout the entire state, and

---

3   Ibid.

other states throughout the US followed suit, such as Georgia, South Carolina, Virginia, North Carolina, and Kentucky.

Real estate brokers and White owners of property located in mixed communities voiced their concerns about the ordinance. There wasn't any concern in reference to the discrimination of Black people, but about how it would potentially stop their cash flow. They feared forthcoming vacant issues, because if White people move out of their homes away from the Blacks who moved in before the ordinance, then who's to say those vacancies will ever be filled again, if the law prohibits it?

There was a second ordinance that corrected legal flaws in the first, to benefit the racist and whiny real estate brokers and White owners of property—making it inapplicable to "mixed blocks": "All-Black blocks were to remain all-Black, all-White blocks were to remain all-White, and integrated blocks were left to pursue their market destiny."[4]

Power also reveals to us a study from 1933 that found Baltimore's "blighted" areas in which the physical condition of dwellings was below the standard for rehabilitation, with substantial health and sanitary problems, and which were predominantly populated by Blacks (they took care of the White blocks and not the Black): "These districts received few municipal services. Garbage and refuse went uncollected. Alleys were infested with rats. The sewer system had been completed in 1914, but many houses in the 17th Ward were still not connected; it is said that building inspectors were bribed. When toilets were installed, in some small houses there was so little space they were placed next to the front door. The vast majority of the Negro population continued to live under unsanitary conditions, to infect one

---

4   Ibid.

another, and to spread communicable diseases to the broader community."[5]

Laws were in place that, if you broke them, would result in you being sentenced to a fine, jail time, or both. It is a metaphor for why police officers act the way that they do in our communities. The policies and laws of this land are what shape the culture of policing. It is their job, their sworn duty, to uphold that law, and they bend the law for White people, and themselves, and crack down double when Black people are involved.

Since racist laws aren't as cut and dry as they were decades ago, racists who crave the need to dominate and control who lives in their neighborhoods and occupies their spaces take it upon themselves to do so.

On May 25, 2020, Melody Cooper posted a video on YouTube, which her brother, Christian Cooper, recorded. Christian asked a woman to "put her dog on the leash," in an area in Central Park where it was required of dog owners. The White women, Amy Cooper, who was asked to follow the laws of the park, got violent, pulled out her cell phone, and said, "I'm going to tell them that there is an African American man threatening my life," before calling the police. According to NBC New York, Amy apologized and mentioned, "When I think about the police, I'm such a blessed person," she said. "I've come to realize especially today that I think of [the police] as a protection agency, and unfortunately, this has caused me to realize that there are so many people in this country that don't have that luxury."[6] It's not

5 Ibid.
6 Price, Brian, et al. "Woman in Racial Central Park Confrontation Is Fired From Job, Gives Up Dog." NBC New York, May 27, 2020, https://www .nbcnewyork.com/news/local/central-park-confrontation-goes-viral -white-woman-calls-cop-on-black-birder/2431773/.

protection, because she is not being harmed. The Internet called this woman "Karen," which has become a label for problematic White women initiating and pursuing racial and violent behavior in public places toward Black people. I believe that we should leave the term "Karen" on the playground and call them what they are—White women exercising racist, violent, and deadly behavior.

Assigning racist nicknames belittles the damage they can do, I believe. Amy explicitly mentioned Christian's race with the intent for the police to come and arrest or murder him. The mentioning of his race automatically makes Amy Cooper an agent of the state, knowingly or unknowingly. These videos of White women calling the police are easy to find on the Internet, so I won't waste any time linking you to them but, instead, will cover the history of why this is our reality.

Former FBI Director J. Edgar Hoover made the FBI a source of pride for White Americans, and a nightmare for Black. In a notation found in the book *I Am Not Your Negro*, James Baldwin indicated a quote by Hoover: "We all should be concerned with but one goal: the eradication of crime. The Federal Bureau of Investigation is as close to you as your nearest telephone. It seeks to be your protector in all matters within its jurisdiction. It belongs to you."[7]

Racists being able to utilize their phones to eliminate Black bodies is their most reliable connection to the state, and to their White privilege. If White women can't control a situation, traditionally they go to their husbands, or some type of male figure in their life to "handle," "control," or "eliminate" the situation. If those men are not available to them in their proximity, the state then becomes their men. This is an example of White privilege

---

7 Baldwin, James. *I Am Not Your Negro*, Vintage (New York 2017).

and White power—having the luxury to be able to use the state as a resource to eliminate something that is uncomfortable for them. You want Black children out of your pool? You don't want people barbecuing in a public park? You don't want Black people entering an apartment building in which they live? You call the police. This is the epitome of racism, White privilege, and White supremacy. White people using their phones is a new Jim Crow tactic of intimidation, that has destroyed the personal freedom of Black Americans in this country, many times leading to violent deaths.

Some people will try and excuse the behavior of the Amy Coopers of the world by saying, "But, what if she was really scared, and that's why she called the police?" People's perceptions are very real to them; however, they need to ask themselves, "Why am I scared?" and, "What is my fear based on?"

Some months back I was a part of an online Instagram discussion with some Maryland Institute College of Art (MICA) students in regard to my book *Hummingbirds in the Trenches*. We were discussing everything from my writing to community work. One of the students in the comment section said, "There are very few people who are actually willing to venture into areas they have been told are unsafe. Fidel expressed for the lives and future boys raised in Baltimore. . . . We as college students in the area are told to fear those same boys."

In an essay titled "Cinderella's Stepsisters," from her book, *The Source of Self-Regard*, Toni Morrison wrote:

In your rainbow journey towards the realization of personal goals, don't make choices based only on your security and your safety. Nothing is safe. That is not to say that anything ever was, or anything worth achieving ever should be. The things of value seldom are. It is not safe to

have a child. It is not safe to challenge the status quo. It is
not safe to choose work that has not been done before. Or
old work in a new way. Don't let your safety diminish the
safety of your stepsister.[8]

In his book *Stamped From the Beginning*, Ibram X. Kendi details,
"Drunk drivers, who routinely kill more people than violent
urban Blacks, were not regarded as violent crimes in such studies, and 78 percent of arrested drunk drivers were White males
in 1990. In 1986, 1,092 people succumbed to 'cocaine related'
deaths, and there were another 20,610 homicides. That adds
up to 21,702, still lower than the 23,990 alcohol-related traffic
related deaths that year (not to mention the number of serious
injuries caused by drunk drivers that do not result in death).
White drunk drivers were killing other White people at a far
greater rate."[9] Those violent Black faces only existed on their TV
screens and their imaginations.

In other words, racist ideas bamboozled the masses. Inner-
city streets were safer than suburban highways, where innocent
bystanders were murdered, but there was a war on crime and
drugs, and not drunk driving. It shows that J. Edgar Hoover and
everyone who supported his messages in regard to crime didn't
truly want to eradicate crime, but eradicate Black people.

In 2019, seventeen-year-old Dawnta Harris was sentenced
to life in prison after fatally striking Amy Caprio, a police officer,
who was responding to a burglary call in a Perry Hall neighborhood. Investigators said three teens were burglarizing a
home while Harris waited outside in a getaway car, a stolen Jeep

---

8   Morrison, Toni. "Cinderalla's Stepsisters." *The Source of Self-Regard*, Knopf
    (New York 2019).
9   Kendi, Ibram X. *Stamped from the Beginning*, 437–438.

Wrangler. During the trial, a body cam video showed the fatal encounter: Caprio ordered Harris to get out of the car, pulling out her gun. That's when he hit the gas. Harris was tried as an adult and convicted of felony murder, and may not ever see his loved ones again outside of prison bars. In a letter Harris wrote by hand that was read by his defense attorney Warren Brown in court, "I didn't want to hurt her," Harris wrote. "I just felt I was in a life-or-death situation. I wish I could go back to that day and not do what I did."[10]

Former Bishop Heather Cook was driving drunk and texting, which caused her to kill a cyclist, and after, she fled the scene. Cook pleaded guilty and was sentenced to jail in October 2015 for manslaughter, DUI, leaving the scene of an accident, and texting while driving. She was given a ten-year sentence with five years suspended for manslaughter and a ten-year sentence with eight years suspended for traffic violations including leaving the scene. It was not the first DUI for Cook. In 2010, she was charged with multiple offenses including possession of marijuana and DUI, for which she received probation before judgment and a $300 fine.[11]

Police in Caroline County brought those charges after an officer pulled Cook over on a traffic stop; there was no crash or injury involved. She described the living conditions "bleak and cold," and while incarcerated, she got married in 2017 to her

---

10 Hellgren, Mike. "'I Didn't Want To Hurt Her': Dawnta Harris Sentenced To Life In Prison In Ofc. Amy Caprio's Death." CBS Baltimore, August 21, 2019, https://baltimore.cbslocal.com/2019/08/21/dawnta-harris-sentencing -teen-convicted-amy-caprio-death-baltimore-county-police/.

11 Banks, Adelle M. "Once a bishop, now a 'poster child' for alcoholism, Heather Cook seeks to make amends." ReligionNews.com, May 14, 2019, https://religionnews.com/2019/05/14/once-a-bishop-now-a-poster-child -for-alcoholism-heather-cook-seeks-to-make-amends/.

partner, a fellow recovering alcoholic who lives on the Eastern Shore, Religion News Service reported. They met while in the seminary.

Cook, who was the first female bishop in Maryland, was elected the second-highest-ranking official in the Episcopal Diocese of Maryland in May 2014. Cook was released early in 2019 because she had earned credits for good behavior, including working in the prison's mail room, holding recovery meetings for those suffering from addiction, and organizing recovery summits at the prison, the *Baltimore Sun* reported.[12]

What's the comparison between Dawnta and Cook? Cook was a violent repeat offender, regularly putting innocent people's lives in danger. But, because she's White, her privilege afforded her the space to murder someone, and get out of prison early, and she still was able to pursue a meaningful love life because "White people make mistakes," and it's not in Cook's White inherent nature to do such a thing. Racist ideas persuade the masses to believe that because Dawnta is Black, he's inherently hypermasculine, violent, and criminal, and doesn't make "mistakes," because of his inheritance of savagery. Racist ideas are what justified the judge's decision to give him a life sentence— no matter how young he was and how malleable his mind at his age.

This world tells people what and who to fear. We, all of us, do unsafe things all the time. We almost always do every bad thing that our parents tell us not to do—things that could kill us, such as driving without seat belts, riding bicycles without

---

12 Pitts, Jonathan M. "Ex Bishop Released from Prison after Serving Half of Sentence for Fatal Drunk Driving Crash, May 14, 2019, https://www.baltimoresun.com/maryland/baltimore-city/bs-md-cook-released-20190513-story.html.

helmets, indulging in alcohol and drugs, drinking and driving, texting and driving. And then you have the risk-takers, who go skydiving, or who stick their hands in mouths of shark.

You have to ask yourself, "Am I afraid of the unsafe, or am I afraid of Black people?" If you interrogate your own thoughts, and realize that you are not afraid of the unsafe but are in fact afraid of Black people, that's your own internalized racism, and it's no one else's duty to alleviate that fear by making you feel comfortable. The work is for you to do.

Fuck the Police

"Fuck the police" has been a popular phrase in my community for as long as I can remember. My favorite rappers rapped it over instrumentals, dirt-bike riders in my neighborhood kicked cop cars and spat on them as they skirted off wheelie'n, and my father said, "Fuck the police," as if it were his second language. One day my father came to my house and told me to walk with him to the store so he could grab us some cold-cut subs and half and halfs from one of the delis inside of Northeast Market. As we hiked up Jefferson Street, we both stopped in the alley to take a piss. As soon as we were finishing, a cop car pulled up to the alley, we were in the middle, my father said, "C'mon Koni, let's go," and we cut through alleyways and side streets to escape the cop car, all the way until we made it inside of Northeast Market. I'm surprised my nine-year-old legs could keep up. My father was out of breath and said, "Man, fuck the police. They will lock you up for anything. Can't even drain the weasel in peace." I remember one morning I was lying on the living room floor watching *Hey Arnold* and *Rugrats*, when the police burst through my front and back doors, with their guns pointed at everything breathing. They arrested my father for allegedly flushing some heroin down the toilet, but as they walked him out in cuffs, he said, "Fuck y'all," to all of them and chastised them for disturbing me and my grandmother's peace. When both my mother and father were in prison at Jessup Correctional Facility, as a youngin' I remember the prison guards were always angry, and by the way they ill-treated the prisoners, you could tell they hated them just as much as they hated their jobs.

Without cursing, as a kid, I'd ask my father why we didn't like the police, and why they routinely harassed us without "reasoning." I remember him saying, "It's because we're Black," and I don't recall him providing any context other than that.

My father told me several stories about Baltimore City police as a kid, but the ones that stuck with me the most were the stories about getting harassed by them, and about "crazy racist White boys," while he and his friends minded their business, playing in Patterson Park. He told me that it was always one or the other terrorizing them. They got called everything from monkeys to "ain't shit little niggers," and many times it involved them getting beat up by the cops, or the "crazy racist white boys," chasing them out of the park with baseball bats. Patterson Park is located in East Baltimore and was established in 1827—named after William Patterson, a wealthy shipping merchant who donated six acres of land—becoming the oldest park in Baltimore. Before it was an official park, the site played a major role in the Battle of Baltimore during the war of 1812, being an essential position for US forces against the British. Blacks served on both sides of this war, which was used as an opportunity to secure freedom, and hopes of providing a better life for their families. Enslaved Blacks faced some tough decisions because British Vice Admiral Alexander Cochrane issued a proclamation aimed toward enslaved Black men across the Chesapeake region—and by joining the British military, runaway slaves had an opportunity to relocate to a British colony as free citizens. This is one of many instances where Blacks sacrificed their lives, for the betterment of a country that gave them nothing in return but discrimination.

It was nothing more poetic than me being a youngin', and having troubles with the law, in this same exact park that my father once did. One night my friends and I were sitting at Luzerne Avenue, the block where most of us lived, four blocks away from the park. For us, the park was a hub for pick-up basketball games and swimming, and the park hosted Virginia S. Baker, a recreation center where my cousin and I attended summer camp as kids. But on this particular day we had different plans for how we would deal with the park, just as the park had different plans for us. My homie Mark had just gotten released from a juvenile detention center a few days prior to our gathering and was venting to us about his difficulties in finding work, and about his family disowning him because of his reoccurring run-ins with the police, on top of dropping out of school. He pulled three black medal BB guns out of his backpack and sat them on the marble steps.

"Yo, you see these? They look real, don't they?"

"Hell yeah."

"Exactly, so if we catch somebody slippin' down the park, ain't nobody gonna crack slick. It's like ten of us."

We agreed. I took one of the guns, Mark had one, and our homie Ryheem had the other. The rest of the gang marched with us just in case we had to get physical with someone resisting the stick-up. We touched all bases of the park and ran into absolutely no one. We realized we were on a dead mission and decided to walk back home. As we made our way back to Luzerne, lights and police sirens lit up the park, and we made the smart decision to toss the BB guns and run. Some of the homies had lighting for feet and got away—if you were behind them, all you saw was ass and elbows. Cop cars sliced through the grass, and before I know it, five of us had police boots on our throats. The cops stomped our stomach and ribs and called us pieces of shit as they handcuffed us. They tossed us in the paddy wagon and ignored us as we asked them why we were being arrested. Once we arrived at the police station, they told us that we were being charged for assaulting a Hispanic male and robbing him of $500 and his moped. Later that next day, my grandmother picked me up from the station, cursed me out, and scolded me about making right decisions in my life, and how I'll end up like my parents if I don't. She didn't believe me when I told her that we didn't do what the police said we did. She didn't believe me but was glad that I was home, nonetheless. Fast-forward to our first, and last, court date regarding this alleged assault and robbery. Neither the arresting officers, nor the alleged Hispanic male that was involved, showed up to court, so the judge dropped the charges and allowed me and my homies to walk. Still to this day, I think about the outcome and my future, and wonder if they had showed up to court, what would that have looked like for us? Would we still be incarcerated? If convicted, in what ways would it have threatened our future employment? School? College? Would we have been able to attend things like graduation? How about prom? One of the most anticipated days of my high school career was almost ruined by Baltimore City police.

* * *

It was my senior year of high school, and it was my prom day. I was rushing to get dressed, after oversleeping during my nap. I threw on my clothes, slapped on my cologne, brushed my teeth, washed my face, and headed out the front door, searching for my cousin who was supposed to be riding with me. He had said he was going to the corner store "real quick," which I should've known was a lie. About five minutes later, he came around the corner with a black bag filled with snacks, "You ready?"

"Yeah, I'm ready. Come on, dummy, we gotta hurry up."

We hopped in the car, banged a right on Orleans Street, and headed toward my prom date's house, where we'd have the official leaving celebration. After cruising a few blocks, we got stopped by the police. Our lives didn't matter to them, so of course, they didn't care about me being dressed for prom and had no problem with ruining a special day for me and my family. They yanked all of us out of the car and forced us on the ground—they said they had probable cause to search our vehicle because they saw my cousin purchase some marijuana before getting in the car and driving off. Of course, they lied, because that's what Baltimore City police specialize in. On top of it all, my cousin never touched a drug before in his life—for use or distribution. Baltimore police have a strong reputation for planting both drugs and guns on people; however, this time they let us slide after checking the car and not "finding" anything.

Another time, I was riding my bicycle to the store, and when I approached the corner of Rose Street and Orleans Street, police hopped out of their cars, detained me, and I was searched by two officers. Their reason being that riding a bike on the sidewalk was illegal. After searching my name in the system, they harassed me even more as I sat on the curb, after finding out that my father and I had the same name. "Oh, you don't look like you was born in the seventies." And, "Oh this is Fuzzy's son." And, "Don't end up like that motherfucker." I can't count the many times I've had the Gun Trace Task Force (a so-called "elite" squad of "highly trained" officers tasked with seizing illegal guns) roll up on me and my friends with their guns out, slamming us against walls and cop cars, digging in our private areas, in search of guns and drugs that we didn't have on us. Or the time where I was arrested for loitering while running store errands for my grandmother. Back then, my friends and I didn't know what "constitutional rights" were, let alone knew that they were being violated.

When I propose that we as a country should defund the police, and abolishing them being our end goal, it's not because of a personal vendetta I have for police because of how they terrorized my friends and me, it's because racist cops arrest, ruin the lives of, and murder Black people throughout this country constantly.

In 2018, eight of those "elite" and "highly trained" police were convicted on charges of racketeering, conspiracy, multiple violent robberies, and overtime fraud. In 2017, Mayor Catherine Pugh ordered a forensic audit of police overtime, and during that time it was discovered to be $1.6 million every two weeks, which is $40 million in overtime yearly. Back in 2014, the *Baltimore Sun* reported that since 2011 city police officers have faced 317 lawsuits for civil rights and constitutional violations, such as false imprisonment, assault, and false arrest. The *Sun* investigation also showed that even though the city had paid out $5.7 million over that period in lawsuits, it was revealed that the police leaders, city attorneys, and other top officials weren't keeping track of the officers who repeatedly faced lawsuits with allegations of brutality, which allowed them to continue to use their power to steal money, drugs, and guns and plant drugs and guns on citizen to further their terrorization. The entire state needs to be held accountable for its participation and aiding in the terror of Baltimore citizens that was carried out by police. One of the many repeated criminals was former Baltimore Police Det. Daniel Hersl, who was convicted and sentenced to eighteen years in prison in 2018 for his role in the task force's illegal and deadly series of schemes, and his overtime fraud. In my neighborhood, if Hersl didn't beat your ass before, then you knew someone who got their ass beaten by him. His reputation of being a thief, abusive, and a certified cruddy individual is not just "He-says-she-says." Before this GTTF investigation, Hersl had cost the city $200,000 in lawsuit settlements. He was accused of everything from breaking a guy's nose and jaw, to beating up and arresting a woman who was selling church raffle tickets.

Even more recently, on June 25, 2020, a Baltimore City police sergeant by the name of James Lloyd had a dispute with his patio contractor that ended up in Lloyd kidnapping and robbing him. The patio contractor sorted out a price quote for Lloyd for $7,000 to build a patio. Lloyd wanted the patio to be larger, and the contractor gave him the price of $1,400 for the add-on. Lloyd was upset, and knowing that his police badge and gun grant him the power to terrorize and steal, he arrived at the patio contractor's home and invited three of his homicide detectives to join. Lloyd and his cruddy buddies had their badges and guns out, Lloyd threatened the man, told him his license was suspended, and they'd he'd have him arrested and his car towed. The patio instructor said that the guns, arrest threats, and the police aggressive tones scared him. Lloyd then drove him to the bank and made him take out a $3,500 cashier's check, while Lloyd held the man's license the entire time. Lloyd is charged with extortion and kidnapping, while his three accomplices are on administrative duty pending an investigation.

Imagine if the police didn't get caught? The average person in America can't afford to have $3,500 taken from them. Imagine if Lloyd and his crew didn't get caught, and how this could literally destroy a family. Baltimore City police have stolen lesser amounts of money than this from people I know. And I've heard stories where people went into debt, lost homes and cars, because of the thieves with badges.

The violent history of Baltimore City police, and the terror-ization of Baltimore residents, stretches for eons, and although merely a spec of America's issues, it is a reflection of the violent history of policing in this country, and why they need to be abolished.

* * *

On August 1, 2016, I was scrolling through Instagram and kept seeing pictures of a beautiful woman accompanied by the hashtags #KorrynGaines #CityForever. I searched the hashtags and discovered 23-year-old Korryn Gaines, a Baltimore City native who also walked the same hallways with me at Baltimore City College High School. Baltimore County Police invaded Korryn's home, gunned her down, and shot her son—all for an arrest warrant related to a traffic stop. It was a devastating time for Baltimore, City High Community, and the Black community as a whole.

A few days later, just after performing at a local open mic in Baltimore, I went home, napped, and woke up to a few missed calls and a voice mail.

"Good morning Kondwani, this is Aleisha calling at 10:00 a.m. on August 4th. We are getting some things together for Korryn Gaines's candlelight vigil at 7:00 p.m. tomorrow at City High School. We wanted you to attend as a guest speaker or maybe do a poem or something. If that's something you are up for, then give me a call back. Again, this is Aleisha. Bye."

I returned Aleisha's call and accepted.

I pulled up to my alma mater for Korryn's vigil, put my van in park, took a small sip of mango Amsterdam, and my phone rang. "Yo, Kon. Where you at? It's your time to speak." I hung up the phone with Aleisha and then went on to give my speech, in which I addressed the issue of violent racist police, among other things.

I listened to Korryn's family and friends speak about how good a person and mother she was. Her father, Ryan Gaines Sr., said that during the hours-long standoff, he and other family members asked to go in and get Korryn out of the house because they were certain she would listen to them. The police responded, "It's far beyond that now." The term "far beyond that now" was confirmation that those bullets had "Korryn Gaines" engraved on them before the standoff even had begun—she was dead long before they arrived at her home. In 2018, a grand jury had awarded $38 million to Korryn's family, who sued Baltimore County Police for wrongful death, but the decision was reversed the following year by the circuit court judge, who hailed the officers who murdered Korryn for "carrying out their duties." There was a recent ruling that claimed the judge was wrong, and her family has won this case and will be granted the $38 million.

At the time Korryn was murdered, videos of her surfaced on the Internet, where she was speaking out about injustices Black people have to deal with in this country. During her traffic stop on March 10, 2016, you could hear her verbally resisting the officers harassing her: "When you put your hands on me. You will have to murder me. You will have to kill me. I promise you. . . . I'm not complying to your criminal fucking ways! I'm not gonna do it!" (The full video can be found on YouTube.)

In 2015 Sandra Bland, a twenty-eight-year-old Black woman, was stopped and arrested by police in Texas for failing to signal a lane change. Three days later, she was found hanging in her cell. Sandra Bland was harassed and pulled over by police for failing to signal a lane change but was abused, arrested, and murdered by the cops because she called them "bullshit," "bitches," and "pussies."

Dr. Zoe Spencer, a professor at Virginia State University, was recently nominated for an Emmy Award for a spoken word performance titled "Say Her Name." Dr. Spencer is not only one of my mentors, but she's also like an aunt to me. Dr. Spencer shared with me an essay she wrote titled "Sassy Mouths, Unfettered Spirits, and the Neo Lynching of Korryn Gaines and Sandra Bland." In this piece she carefully conceptualizes what she calls "Post Traumatic Slave Master Syndrome," and the familiar "policing" of Black Women's Resistance in 21st Century America.

Early in the piece, Dr. Spencer, introduces readers to a few Black women who were viewed threats to White supremacy and were brutally murdered for it in the early 1900s. One of the women was Laura Nelson, who was being held in a local jail on charges of murdering a sheriff. While in jail, she was labeled an "unruly Negro woman" and "bad" for allegedly attempting to grab the gun of a jail guard. During the night before her hearing, she was snatched out of jail by a mob of forty White men and hanged from a bridge to a large White crowd.

On March 31, 1914, two drunken White men broke into the house of Marie Scott and attempted to viciously rape her. Her brother heard her screams and defended his home and his sister, shooting and killing one assailant. When "law enforcement" could not find Scott's brother, they kidnapped Marie Scott from her home instead, placing her in jail. Later that night, a mob of "a dozen or more" White men snatched seventeen-year-old Marie Scott from jail and hanged her from a light pole.

Korryn Gaines and Sandra Bland, among countless unnamed Black women throughout history, fit into the historical pattern of them committing the same crime: being Black in America, and resisting White supremacy. Black women who resist White supremacy are the biggest threats, because to a racist, silencing a Black women's "loud mouth" is a means of social control.

Dr. Spencer tells the reader that these early 1900s violent murders reveal "the historic pattern of lynchings of Black women and girls in America," and how these lynching narratives illustrate the pattern of "white vengeance/retaliation/domination and the savage means that were utilized to silence Black women's voices, control any form of perceived resistance, and utilize fear and coercion to solidify control and establish and sustain racial and gendered power relations."[1]

Even if you don't fit into the "sassy mouth," resisting White supremacy narrative, then you can still fit into that historical context of violent police murdering Black people for just existing, like our beloved Breonna Taylor, who we lost on March 13, 2020. On that day Louisville Metro Police barged into Taylor's home after obtaining a no-knock warrant and fired off more than twenty bullets, killing Taylor. The police claimed to be searching for Taylor's ex-boyfriend, who did not live at Taylor's home, not to mention he was already in police custody. There has been no arrest or charges so far in Taylor's shooting death. Another Black life lost at the hands of killer cops, while our systems are not holding them accountable.

* * *

According to Mapping Police Violence.org,[2] there were only twenty-seven days in 2019 where police did not kill someone. Black people are three times more likely to be killed by the police than white people. Ninety-nine percent of killings by police officers from 2013 to 2019 have not resulted in officers being charged

---

1   Spencer, Zoe, and Perlow, Olivia N. "Sassy Mouths, Unfettered Spirits, and the Neo-Lynching of Korryn Gaines and Sandra Bland: Conceptualizing Post Traumatic Slave Master Syndrome and the Familiar 'Policing' of Black Women's Resistance in Twenty-First-Century America," Meridians, September 1, 2018, https://read.dukeupress.edu/meridians/article-abstract/17/1/163/135606/Sassy-Mouths-Unfettered-Spirits-and-the-Neo?redirectedFrom=fulltext.

2   https://mappingpoliceviolence.org.

with a crime. Police are killing more people so far in 2020 than they did during this period in the past years.

February 2, 2020, a bloodthirsty Wauwatosa, Wisconsin, cop by the name of Joseph Mensah murdered seventeen-year-old Alvin Cole outside of Mayfair mall in Milwaukee, after he allegedly charged officers with a sword and wouldn't drop it. During the upheaval of Cole's murder it was revealed that three families had to bury their loved ones who died at the hands of Mensah. Antonio Gonzales (29) was murdered on July 16, 2015, after being shot eight times by Mensah, and Jay Anderson (25) died on June 23, 2016, after being shot six times. Both of these fatal shootings were deemed justified, and Mensah was not disciplined within his department. Not only were Mensah's murders ruled as justified, he was rewarded a Medal of Valor from Wauwatosa Police Chief Barry Weber for the shooting of Gonzales.[3]

Around 12:30 a.m. on June 2, 2020, Jarrett Tonn, a Vallejo, California, police officer, shot and murdered twenty-two-year-old Sean Monterrosa, after alleging he had a gun, when it was just a hammer. Tonn shot five times through the windshield of his cop car at Monterrosa, killing him. According to the *Mercury News*,[4] the shooting of Monterrosa was Tonn's fourth time in five years

3   Casey, Evan, and Kahugen, Christopher. "Jay-Z's social justice group calls for prosecution of a Wauwatosa officer who has shot and killed three people. Here's what we know." *Journal Sentinel*, July 2, 2020, https://www.jsonline.com/story/communities/west/news/wauwatosa/2020/07/02/wauwatosa-police-officer-mensah-has-killed-three-people-five-years/5356213002/.

4   Gartrell, Nate. "eport contradicts Vallejo police chief's claim in officer's fatal shooting of 22-year-old." *The Mercury News*, June 10, 2020, https://www.mercurynews.com/2020/06/10/report-sean-monterrosa-was-declared-dead-an-hour-after-being-shot-by-vallejo-officer-contradicting-chiefs-public-statement/.

firing his gun while on duty, including two shootings within six weeks in 2017, and a shooting in 2015 where he fired eighteen times. None of the three prior shootings resulted in a death; internal investigations cleared Tonn of wrongdoing each time.

Whether or not you partake in "criminal" activities, this country will find a way to murder you, or throw you behind bars, if you are Black. And if you are White, they will try their best to keep you out of jail. Policies and laws shape policing in this country.

Ethan Couch, a White sixteen-year-old, was sentenced to ten years of probation in 2013 for a drunk driving crash that killed four people, and injured two. The prosecutor urged that Couch should receive twenty years; however, because he's White and rich, he did no jail time because a psychologist testified that Couch was a victim of "affluenza," which he blamed for Couch's dangerously violent lifestyle, which is attributed to his affluent upbringing and irresponsible parenting. While on probation, Couch violated it, which sparked a manhunt that discovered he and his mother had fled to Mexico. They were both arrested, extradited to the US, and served 720 days in prison, and were released in April 2018 on probation. January 2020, Couch was back in jail after violating probation again, testing positive for THC in a mandatory drug screening.

A white rapist by the name of Brock Turner was found guilty of three felony accounts after raping a woman at Stanford University. In March 2016, a jury found him guilty of assault with intent to commit rape of an intoxicated or unconscious person, penetration of an intoxicated person, and penetration of an unconscious person.

The victim self-disclosed and said Brock raped her. There were also two individuals who saw him behind a dumpster, half-naked, taking advantage of this unconscious woman. The judge cut him some "slack" due to his lack of criminal history and his show of remorse. The judge forgot to mention his biggest escape, which was one's most valuable asset in America: white skin. After a prosecutor argued he should spend six years in prison, the judge ruled he should be jailed for six months. His White privilege struck again, and he only did three months and was released in September of 2016. The judge said, "A prison sentence would have a severe impact on him."[5] I wish some judges would've spared my friends and family, but because of our Blackness, it's a no-go.

If Black people got the luxury of judges "sparing time" because jail has "severe impacts" on all human beings, and not just White people, other kids and I wouldn't wake up with brick-heavy tear ducts, thinking about our parents and friends who vanished from our neighborhoods into prison cells—sometimes for life.

In 1990, Jonathan Fleming was convicted and arrested for the murder of his friend Daryl Rush in New York. Fleming argued that he was on a vacation at Disney World during the time his friend Rush was murdered in 1989. Despite Fleming's evidence of videos, post cards, and a plane ticket to Florida, the prosecution argued that he could have flown back to New York, killed Rush, and returned to Disney World. A witness testified to seeing Fleming commit the murder. Later on, the witness admitted to falsely accusing him to get her own charges dropped. The prosecutors said she was lying, so they ignored her claim. In 2013, the case reopened, and in 2014, after spending over two decades in prison, Fleming was released and exonerated: new evidence showed that he was in Florida hours before the murder took place. Fleming's black skin robbed him of over twenty years of his life.

---

5   Stack, Liam. "Light Sentence for Brock Turner in Stanford Rape Case Draws Outrage." *New York Times*, June 6, 2016, https://www.nytimes .com/2016/06/07/us/outrage-in-stanford-rape-case-over-dueling-state -ments-of-victim-and-attackers-father.html.

In 2010, Kalief Browder, a Black sixteen-year-old, was arrested and charged with a robbery that he did not commit. This resulted in him spending three years on Rikers Island, waiting for a trial that never happened. Browder spent two of those years in solitary confinement, where he was cramped in windowless rooms for twenty-four-hour days, which inflicted him with psychological pain. When he did have contact with humans, it was brutal. He was beaten by inmates and correctional officers regularly. He attempted suicide on several occasions while incarcerated. A few months after he was released in 2013, innocent, he attempted suicide again. Browder was in and out of psychiatric hospitals, until he later got the job done in June 2015. It's no doubt that his traumatic experiences at Rikers Island were the cause of his mental instability, which resulted in him taking his own life. Another murder of a Black person with America's blood all over it.

Martin Luther King, Jr., once said, "A just law is a man-made code that squares with the moral law, or the law of God. An unjust law is a code that is out of harmony with the moral law." Many laws that are enforced by this system play a key role in the execution of Black people in America. If I shoot and kill someone, I will get charged with murder and do a prison sentence that probably would jail me for the rest of my life. However, White police officer Betty Shelby murdered Terence Crutcher, a Black man, in Tulsa, Oklahoma, while he had his hands up. She was charged with manslaughter in the first degree. Betty did twenty minutes in jail and was released on $50,000 bail.[6]

---

6   Sidahmed, Mazin. "Tulsa police officer released on $50,000 bail in Terence Crutcher shooting." The Guardian, September 23, 2016, https://www.theguardian.com/us-news/2016/sep/23/terence-crutcher-shooting-tulsa-officer-betty-shelby-bail.

When we talk about legal and illegal, remember, the enslavement and murder of Africans in America was legal at a point in history but is against the "law" now. One of the most impactful loopholes to sustain Black enslavement, murder, and oppression in America is the 13th Amendment, which reads, "The United States Constitution abolished slavery and involuntary servitude, except as punishment for a crime." This then created justification for a new slavery, by labeling Black people as criminals and creating racist policies and ideas so that we are again enslaved. Once again creating false perceptions that there is something wrong with Black people, and not the system.

Pew Research Center studies show that in 2018, Black Americans represented 33 percent of the sentenced prison population, nearly triple their 12 percent share of the US adult population. Whites accounted for 30 percent of prisoners, about half their 63 percent share of the adult population.[7] If Black people make up 12 percent of the US population, then that means we should account for somewhere close to 12 percent of the inmates in the US prisons. Racial disparities?

When Black and Brown people go to prison, they now provide free labor, which is the prison industrial complex. These prisons are privatized, therefore corporations are able to profit from the free labor of the prisoners, while the taxpayers are paying for their incarceration. When we are discussing the enslavement of Black people in this country, there is much more money to be made from labor now in prisons than during slavery.

Today, prisons and corporations get a double benefit

---

7   Gramlich, John. "Black imprisonment rate in the U.S. has fallen by a third since 2006." Pew Research Center, May 6, 2020, https://www.pewresearch.org/fact-tank/2020/05/06/black-imprisonment-rate-in-the-u-s-has-fallen-by-a-third-since-2006/.

because prison is free labor, and it's 100 percent profit because they don't have to pay for housing, and food, as slave owners did during slavery. It benefits them, that's why they create laws that will imprison people who look like me. It's beneficial to create laws that promote mass incarceration. They will do whatever they can within their power to put you behind bars so they can exploit your free labor. Then you work for all of them years, just to come out, and it is almost impossible for you to find work so you can provide for your survival. Not your wants, but your needs. This then prompts people to find quicker ways to get money illegally—working jobs where you get paid under the table or even selling drugs, or selling inspection sticker tags (some of the things I've seen people do). Now you will go back into the system.

There are laws that protect White people like Brock Turner and Ethan Couch so they don't get arrested, or if they do, their whiteness grants them a privilege to serve lesser prison sentences than Blacks, because for us, criminality is the rule, and for them, it's the exception. Thus, if I ever get arrested, the assumption is that I'm naturally a criminal, so when I come out, if I do, no one will give me a chance. But if someone like a Brock gets locked up, he has an opportunity to get back on his feet and do well in society. Brock made a mistake (no matter how horrible it was), so we're gonna give him a second chance because that's not in his inherent nature. We're doing society a justice by not sending Brock to jail, so he won't be like the criminally "inherent" Black folks.

History shows that it is this country's duty to utilize its institutions to enslave, murder, and oppress Black people, without repercussions. Too many conversations when dealing with police killing Black people involve the statement "Well, what did he or she do?" Because we are conditioned to believe that there is something wrong with Black people, these murders become normal and become the fault of the victim and not the killer. Of course, until we reach a place in this country where we abolish police, I believe any police officer who unjustly murders civilians should be charged and convicted for murder. If they don't do time in jail but instead get desk leave duty, they should have to work for free until they retire, and the money they would have received should go to the family of the victim. Money can't replace a lost life; however, I believe that it would be a step toward holding cops accountable for the murders they commit. Also, the lawsuits that comes out of taxpayers' dollars should instead be paid by the cop, and (or) their district.

If I have the opportunity to have children one day in the future—even if by then policing is in fact abolished—best believe I will tell my kids, it's forever, "fuck the police."

If you voted or advocated for laws to mass-incarcerate Black people, or you enable the violence inflicted on Black people by the police, you need to reflect and be vocal and honest about all of the ways you participated in the destroying of Black people's lives and opportunities.

Police leaders, city attorneys, and other top officials who have not been monitoring the violent behavior of the Baltimore City cops, allowing them to plague our streets, terrorize and murder Black citizens—y'all need to be vocal about how you participated and push toward the prosecution of all officers who have been involved in the terrorization of the people, and if you can't bring yourself to do that, then respectfully step down from your positions.

I believe that one quantifiable way to start defunding the police departments across the country is by channeling money to Historically Black College and Universities (HBCUs). The money can be used to hire educators who would be employed by the universities and would teach community members interested in taking the place of police officers, and who could be called for intercommunal issues that don't require (or permit) a gun and badge. They pursue certifications as mental health, de-escalation, and community engagement specialists. So the HBCUs would receive more funding, while teaching community members skills they can use in and outside of work, and I believe this can be a pivotal part in the movement to eradicate the police in America.

Turn the Fire Down

C hristmas season, all across America, is hailed as the most wonderful time of the year. The time of the year where many put their priorities to the backseat of the happiness of others. Landlords receive late rent payments because tenants' loved ones want the latest NBA 2K, or new Tiffany's jewelry, or tennis shoes. The time of the year where some people borrow money, and give back with interest, or with no real plans of returning it back to the lender. And the time where you enjoy precious and unforgettable moments with your friends and family.

Holiday rituals vary from household to household, but growing up, ours was pretty traditional. Me, my cousin Avon, his mother, and our grandmother would decorate our living room with a Christmas tree filled with ornaments and lights, and with stockings with our names on them that hung on a brown mantel beside the tree—and we had an electric Black Santa Claus that would rock his hips from side to side and sing us Christmas songs. A painting of Jesus hung on the walls above the couch. I could never tell if the thorned-head and bloody-eyed Jesus was Black, or if it was White but just looked Black because the painting was dingy and old. Either way, if it was Black Jesus or dirty White Jesus, he was always there. Even if you forgot about him hanging on the wall, every day someone would refresh your memory of his importance. When crime flooded the news, and all of the "criminals" look just like us. Or if someone survived a tragic incident, it was "won't he do it," he being Jesus, preserving a life. Or if someone hit the lottery it was always "thank you, Jesus!" And every year when we received Christmas gifts, my grandmother and aunt made sure that we thanked Jesus, and Santa Claus, for the huge number of gifts we received.

Around the ages of four to ten are my most vivid memories of the Christmas and New Year holidays as a child. And throughout those years, our household grew a little. My aunt had a little girl who was two years younger than me, and my mother had a baby boy who was six years younger than me. Even when they came into the picture, our rituals stayed intact, and on Christmas Day, we still had enough gifts for five families, flooding our living room and basement. And I remember my grandmother would sit on her favorite couch and sip her Folgers, grinning and watching us open gifts with excitement that she promised she wouldn't get us.

I remember the year that I stopped believing in Santa Claus, I was ten years old. Growing up, I had no problem looking adults in the face and asking them, "If Santa comes in the house through the chimney, and we don't got one, then how he get in our house?" We lived in row homes where a row of attached dwellings share more than just side walls, but mice, arguments, noise, and problems. It didn't take me long to realize adults lie just as much as kids. Well back then I didn't use the word "liar," unless I wanted to get popped in the mouth. I had to say telling stories because if you called someone a liar, my aunt and grandmother took it as calling someone a bitch. I knew that adults were the biggest storytellers when different adults gave me different answers about Santa Claus's home visits to the kids without chimneys. I heard everything from "we leave the door unlocked," to "Santa has a key," to "drops the gifts off out back and we pick them up." But I still believed that maybe, all of them were true.

At ten years old, not only did I start to question Santa, but I started to question everything—even the integrity of adults— and the things they told me, such as "this is just life," in the face of tragedy.

December 31, 2003, it was the early morning. I was sleeping in my room and was awakened by what sounded like a hammer to the front door of our house. Hearing knocking and screaming was pretty normal in my neighborhood, caused by drug addicts and drunks—fighting. And also normal because we live in row homes, where someone could be knocking on a neighbor's door and it would feel like yours. I paid the noise no mind, tried to go back to sleep, and the knocks returned. My grandmother woke up, and I heard her walking toward the steps, she slept in the master bedroom at the front of the house so she could hear the knocking and screaming more clearly. I followed her to the front door, and I bent down and peeped through the small gateway between her arm and the door, and there it was. Thick clouds of carbon black smoke barged out of a bedroom window across the street. I was in shock, and then it hit me. That's the bedroom of my two best friends, little brother Fidel, who was seven, and his older brother, Davon, who was eleven. Y'all mother was running up and down the block screaming at the top of her lungs begging for people to call 911 so that her babies could be rescued. I ran to the house phone that sat on the shelf connected to the china cabinet and called 911, shaking, trembling, crying. "It's a fire on my block. My brothers are in a fire." So shaken I forgot to tell the operator where I lived. I was one of many people who called, so the operator asked, "400 block of Luzerne? We have help on the way." and I hung up.

Went outside. I stood there and watched a house burn down, while y'all were in it. All I kept wishing was that I was the human torch. Begging that God or his son could lend me some powers just for the moment. I also couldn't help but think if our father wasn't in prison during the time, what would he have done? Risked his life to save y'all. I wish I had as much courage as that man did, at ten years old. But I didn't. The firefighters snatched off y'all roof and burst open the windows and they pulled out Fidel, then minutes later Davon. Never in my life have I seen a Black body turn completely pink but there y'all were. I remember y'all mother passing out on the concrete at the site of Fidel being pulled out the window. The news said that one of y'all was hiding under the bed, and one of y'all in a corner— y'all hearts stopped beating and they resuscitated on the ride to the hospital. All that I remember seeing at the scene is a burned picture of you two riding on scooters—and y'all melted tricycle and other toys, and other household items.

Everyone in the neighborhood was talking about y'all. And everyone from friends to adults kept saying that you two would be okay. I stayed up for the remainder of the night, and I geared up to walk to Johns Hopkins to see y'all, and before I left the house, we got word that Davon had passed away. Gone. Isn't coming back. Fidel, still alive, but we had to wait to see him because they were still performing surgeries. And on January 2, I got to visit him. I went to the hospital and waited in a crowded visiting room with family and friends from the neighborhood. I finally got called back to see Fidel, right before my father hopped off of the elevator, handcuffed, accompanied by police in a jumpsuit that read "DOC" on the back. We walked into the room together where Fidel was, or what was left of him: burnt faced, blisters the size of golf balls, the smell of burnt flesh. Your beautiful hair, all gone. I didn't know what to say, but Daddy kept urging me to rub you. Kept telling me to talk to you, because you could hear me. Although the doctors said that you were brain dead, Daddy kept telling me that everything was going to be fine. I remember asking him, "Why did you come home only to see him in the hospital?" And, "Will they let you come back home for the funeral, too?" I was a child, but it didn't take rocket science to see that Fidel's condition was deadly. Hooked up to machines, tubes were in your nostril and mouth. White gauze pads. Swollen eyelids and lips. Your head quadrupled in size. And our cousin took a picture of you, while Grandma Gail, our father's mother, rubbed the top of your head where thick nappy braids used to live. Is it weird that I have the pictures in my phone? And that I often look at it? It's hard seeing you like that, but it's the last time I saw you. It's the last time I touched you. It's the last time I was in your presence. It's the last time I looked in your face and said, "I love you." It was the last time I kissed you. That next day, Grandma Gail broke the news that the plug was pulled.

I was torn. I don't talk about it much, but for a very long time, I felt like I committed a crime. I felt like Fidel's and Davon's deaths were my fault, kinda. Take in account, I'm a ten-year-old child. The night before the fire, I repeatedly asked my grandma, "Can Fidel and Davon stay the night?" She said no, and that I could see them the next day. I knew that my grandmother gave me anything I asked for at that age. It was extraordinary for my grandmother to tell me "no," when I asked for something. My grandmother will tell me no 99 times, but on the 100th time she'll say "yes." I was her Achilles heel. Maybe I should've asked over and over again until my tongue fell out? Maybe I should've snuck them over in the middle of the night? Maybe I should've just stayed the night over there, and the three of us could've died together? But I didn't know that this would be our last night playing. "You can play with y'all tomorrow," what my grandmother said. No one knew that was our last night playing. My last time seeing y'all smiles. My last time picking on you and making fun of your stuttering. My last time hearing your voice. My last time seeing you blink. My last time. That's normal, as an adult, I see the foolishness of staying the night when you live across the street—directly across the street. If you're familiar with the design of row homes in Baltimore, then we lived on the same street. If my address was 440, theirs was 435. I didn't know back then as I know now, my brothers' deaths had nothing to do with them, me, nor their mother. Fidel and Davon both died in the crossfire of poverty.

The fire at Fidel and Davon's house started because the two were burning candles for light, because of unpaid bills. My two brothers are only two examples of a symptom of poverty that has stricken similar communities around the US.

According to the National Fire Protection Association, December is the peak time of the year for home candle fires, January is ranked second, and the top three days for home candle fires are New Year's Day, New Year's Eve, and Christmas. The NFPA also reported that from 2012 to 2016, US fire departments responded to an estimate 8,200 home structure fires that started by candles per year. These fires caused an annual average of 80 deaths, 770 injuries, and $264 million in direct property damage. In 2009, heating equipment was involved in an estimated 58,900 reported home structure fires in the United States, which resulted in 480 civilian deaths, 1,520 civilian injuries, and $1.1 billion in direct property damage, reported by NFPA.[1]

I know there are Black fathers who are present in their children's lives and are credited for much of their children's success.

---

1   National Fire Protection Association, https://nfpa.org.

However, growing up in my neighborhood it was uncommon to see men in charge of their households, of their even being in the household at all. The majority of my friends were raised in single households run by Black women.

The median wealth of a single Black parent household is $5,200, a two Black parent household is $16,000, which is still vastly less than a single-parent White family that makes $35,800. According to Federal Reserve data,[2] the median wealth of Black families is $17,600, compared to the median wealth of White families at $171,000. The house fires that stem from unpaid bills result from families using candles during the winter season for light, and from kerosene space heaters that are more common in low-income areas. Fifty percent or more of their income goes toward housing costs—payment burdens. When all of their money goes toward bills, then there is little left over to provide for their children's needs, and sometimes rent will go unpaid just to see the smiles on children's faces.

Who knows why the gas and electric bill wasn't paid, or whatever, but living in the richest state inside of the US, it shouldn't be that people die because of unpaid bills. We shouldn't live in a world where people get penalized for being both Black and poor. Forbes reported that in 2017, Americans paid $34 billion in overdraft fees. Pretty sure rich people don't pay overdraft fees.[3]

---

2   Dettling, Lisa J. "Recent Trends in Wealth-Holding by Race and Ethnicity: Evidence from the Survey of Consumer Finances." September 27, 2017, https://www.federalreserve.gov/econres/notes/feds-notes/recent-trends -in-wealth-holding-by-race-and-ethnicity-evidence-from-the-survey-of -consumer-finances-20170927.htm.

3   Chang, Julia. "Americans Paid $34 Billion In Overdraft Fees Last Year. Here's How To Stop The Charges." *Forbes*, April 5, 2018, https://www .forbes.com/sites/learnvest/2018/04/05/americans-paid-34-billion-in -overdraft-fees-last-year-heres-how-to-stop-the-charges/#46b65ef73ce9.

Nowadays, I lack excitement during the holidays. I don't care for gifts. I'm not one of those guys who's always screaming how much I hate the holidays, or who tries to throw my energy on others. I'm just pretty quiet and spend time alone for the most part. I do get excitement as I scroll on social media and double-tap pictures and videos of other people enjoying their holidays and traditions—old ones or new ones they've created with their new family. I can't help but think that if I'm fortunate to start my own family one day, which one of your traditions I will steal, and which ones will I create or implement, if any at all.

I believe that as a community, we need to check on our neighbors as best we can during these times.

Mother's Day Deal

During the late 1800s, separate but "equal" laws segregated nearly every aspect of life between Black and White people, ensuring Black inferiority. Because people believed that Blacks were (and still are) "uncivilized," have social "problems," and are "wretched," we therefore deserved to live and die in the slums. We deserve to get educated in the worst schools. And to top everything else, why not just give us drugs to further beat us down?

After drugs were introduced to Black communities throughout this country, Richard Nixon started the war on drugs, only for Ronald Reagan to follow him and double down on this war that gave out mandatory prison sentences for possession of drugs. Even though White people were using and dealing more drugs than Black people, we were still getting harsher jail sentences. If a person got caught with lower-level cocaine, such as crack (which was mainly used and sold in the Black communities), they received a harsher jail sentence than if caught with powder cocaine (which was mainly used and sold by Whites). This is why America can have the largest prison population in the world, and it is mostly filled with

Black people, because Black people are "criminals" and prison is where "criminals" belong.

*　*　*

The sun was blasting. I was at work. Uniform: Nextel Chirp on my hip, Cranberry Nike boots on my feet, Rock & Republic Jeans on my waist, wife beater on my chest. Location: Outside on the corner of Montford and Monument Streets. This isn't your regular 9–5. I was hustlin, of course. Selling dope with my homie, Roc. This is how our little shift worked: I'd take the early morning hitting about 4–5 packs, and have Roc watch the corner for me. Then after I'm done, we'd switch, and I'd watch the corner for Roc. The block was always crowded with the addicts who were our customers as well as everyday people doing everyday things: riding bikes, walking to stores, hanging out with their friends—police periodically lurking.

I was standing on the block scarfing down the last little bit of my frozen cup, and I saw someone walking with hella balloons tied to the back of a stroller. Oh no, I forgot it was Mother's Day. I can't forget a face. I can remember the lyrics to my favorite songs, but I can't remember dates to save my life. I beef with my friends every year because I always forget their birthdays. And if it's not Christmas or Halloween, then forget it.

Holidays don't hold a special place in my heart. But what does hold a special place in my heart is making my grandmother smile, and I know that a Mother's Day gift would do just that. I headed over to CVS to get some last-minute gifts. Getting Mother's Day gifts the day of is hard. None of the stores have any good gifts left, and the stuff that people are selling on the street is way too cheap. So cheap that the phrase "it's the thought that counts" doesn't apply. Most of the Mother's Day aisles are empty, teddy bears scattered all over the store, greeting cards rummaged through—a mess.

While looking amid the wreckage of the card section, I skipped right over the "Mother" area and went straight to "Grandmother." My mother was in prison. A gift probably wouldn't have gotten through.

I found a nice card to put some cash in for Grandma. I found some flowers, a white teddy bear, and three Snickers bars, her favorite candy. I felt like something was missing, so on the way back home I picked up a pack of Newport 100s. It's against the law for fifteen-year-olds to purchase nicotine, but around my way, kids don't abide by the rules, and adults don't enforce them. Some people might say, "Why would you buy your grandmother cigarettes on Mother's Day?" Simple. It's what I felt like doing, and my grandmother loves cigarettes.

Grandma doesn't leave the house, she doesn't wear jewelry anymore, and the clothes that I've bought her in the past, she doesn't wear. I think the changes come with old age. At this point, all she does is glue her body to the couch and her eyes to her Android smartphone, watching ESPN, with a cigarette hanging from the corner of her mouth, right above the mole on her lip.

"Happy Mother's Day," I shouted as I came through the door. When I handed her the goods, it was just how I had pictured, her smile was longer than Wilt Chamberlain's arms. My grandmother's smile was all the proof you needed to see how loving this woman is. When I tell you that my grandmother looks out for everybody, I mean it. I'd give my grandmother the world if I had it, because of how much she does for me, and for others.

My grandmother's name is Mary. People call her Mrs. Mary, Mrs. Phoenix, Mary-Lacy; but me, I just call her Grandma. Because if I call her anything other than that, that's an ass-whooping for seven days straight. Everybody knows my grandmother is the giving queen. I mean, if you need it and she got it, then it's yours. If you need it, and she ain't got it, she gonna go get it, just to give it to you.

Back when Grandma did still leave the house, when I was about ten years old, I remember it was a Sunday morning, which was the day me and Grandma would walk up Monument Street to go to Northeast Market, the only place in my neighborhood that sells semifresh fruits and vegetables. I say "semi" because I've had a few bad apples from there and I've seen a mouse or two, or three, or four. The market is about twelve blocks from my house, but it was the summertime, and the sun made the journey seem longer, and also everyone we passed just couldn't let us walk in peace. "Hey, Mrs. Mary," "How you been, Mrs. Mary?" "I like them shoes, Mrs. Mary," "Mary? Who did your hair girl? I love it." "Oh My God, is that Monique's son? He got so big!" "When Mo coming home? Tell her I asked about her." Like I mentioned before, Mo, my mother, was serving a prison sentence. My mother and grandmother both have been extremely popular in my neighborhood for as long as I can remember.

As soon as we burst through the doors of Northeast Market, it happened all over again. You would've thought my grandmother was some sort of civil rights leader. I grabbed a ticket from the red wheel and stood in the veggie line waiting on our number to be called. There were probably about six to seven people ahead of us. A woman walked up to my grandmother as if she had seen a ghost.

"Mrs. Mary! Mrs. Mary!, I'm so glad I saw you, Mrs. Mary." This was kind of scary. People are usually excited to see my grandmother, but there was something creepy about this woman. This woman looked like she ate twice a week. She had white crust hanging from the corners of her mouth. She looked lost. You could see it all in her eyes.

The lady whispered, "Mrs. Mary, can I please borrow $10? I need it to put towards my groceries." I might be an ignorant little kid, but the way the lady kept shaking and bouncing around, I figured she had to be high on something, or needed to be high on something. My mother had a thing for cocaine and heroin. So I knew firsthand what drug addiction looked like.

My grandmother, being the woman that she is, gave the woman a $20 bill and told her to keep the change. The woman kissed my grandmother on the cheek, said a loud "thank you," and shot to the other side of the market.

That's my grandmother. That's who she is.

That's one of many stories of my grandmother helping others out when they're in need. That's why I love to give back. And that's why I pitched this idea to my homie Roc on how we can show our appreciating for mothers in our neighborhood.

"Yo, let's do something nice for the mothers today."

"What you thinkin'?"

Anybody that's coppin' up, let's charge 'em $7 a pill instead of $10. And we can just buy a half of gallon of the liquor and if they wanna get lit, we can just pour 'em a little bit," I said.

Roc agreed to my day of service idea, so that's what we did.

After a few women came and copped from us, word spread that we had a deal. Business was boomin'. We even had some guys come and try to get the Mother's Day bargain saying things like, "I'm a single parent. I'm the mother and the father." Maybe so, but this deal was for mothers only.

A dangerously skinny woman approached me, with crust on her mouth, and bad nerves. It was the lady from Northeast Market from a few years ago that my grandmother gave $20— she hadn't changed a bit. I handed her two pills and poured her some yak. She guzzled the first cup within seconds and reached out a cup for more. I gave her a second cup and filled both of them until the bottle was gone. The day was coming to an end and I had to get rid of the yak anyway.

"I'm gonna make sure that everybody know about y'all strip. Y'all some nice young men," as she smiled and danced away to the music playing in her head.

I accepted the compliment, wished her a happy Mother's Day, and told her to stay out of trouble.

Just before she walked away, the woman gave me one last snaggle-tooth smile, "Your grandmother raised a nice young man," she declared. "I know she is proud of you!"

Now that made me think. Did my grandmother raise this?

* * *

In Dave Chappelle's Netflix special, *Sticks & Stones,* he discussed the large number of heroin addicts that live in his town in Ohio, comparing today's opioid crisis to the eighties crack epidemic. The most important distinction that was made was the fact that today's opioid crisis gets more attention, and it is seen as a mental health issue because the addicts are White. He gave advice to the White heroin addicts: "hang in there, Whites," he said. "Just say No," quoting Nancy Reagan's antidrug slogan that was prevalent during the eighties and early nineties. "What's so hard about that?" he continued. Chappelle drew attention to the lack of care and racist ideas many people have about Black drug addicts. White people are getting treatment and clinical care for their drug abuse, while we were told to "just say no."

I wish as a child someone would've told me and my friends that drug abuse was a mental health issue, and that our parents were victims of society. It didn't take me until I was an adult to figure this out. Now every time I look up, the opioid epidemic is seen as a mental health crisis because the face of addiction is becoming White. Racist ideas are what made my mother a criminal for her drug addiction, the same addiction for which White people get taken care of and treated like victims.

I wish someone would've told me the hard facts about the history of drug abuse in the Black community, and how we got to this point. People would say, "Don't sell drugs, and don't do drugs." And I'm pretty sure they didn't know any better. My aunt used to try and tell me that my mother was sick, but didn't provide much context as to the underlying causes of drug addiction, and I took it personally and blamed my mother and everyone else who abused drugs. So now, when I speak about drug addiction, I have a proper basis and perspective from which to speak about it in a truthful, non-dehumanizing way. I'll be sure to share with my younger siblings every emotion I went through with our mother and her drug addiction. As I wrote in my poem, "I will tell them":

> I will tell them what it feels like to crawl on miles of cut
> glass
> Just to get the end of the road with bloody palms and
> kneecaps,
> Scars to remind you, that you made it.
> Scars to remind you, that you're human.
> Scars to remind you, that you're strong.
> While your favorite victory song plays in your head, and
> you celebrate.

But I'll also inform them about the history of drug abuse and Black people in this country. I will tell them that being Black comes with a lot of fees written in fine print. I will tell them that drug addiction is the lottery in poverty, and we hit the jackpot for pain, when we don't even play the numbers—and mommy was one of countless individuals who got scratched off. I will tell them that America will give us a treasure chest full of dreams but won't give us a key to take the latch off. Joy Harjo said, "Heroin is a fool offering freedom from the gauntlet of history." Heroin has always been the fool. It's never been my mother. It's never been us.

HBCU LOVE

It was 2011, my senior year of high school, and I hated reading and writing, and didn't see any value in education. Going to college was not a main priority, but I still applied to several universities for two reasons: 1. It was the "next best thing" to do with my life, as everyone was telling me; and 2. I wanted to get away from Baltimore. Two of the colleges I got accepted to were Virginia Union University in Richmond, VA, and Virginia State University, which was thirty minutes down the road in Petersburg, VA. My older cousin Avon was a freshman at Virginia Union at the time, so I asked him for advice on which school I should attend. He persuaded me to attend Virginia State over Virginia Union because they had better resources, a larger student population, and their sporting events were livelier. None of those were of interest to me, and honestly, I wanted to attend school with my cousin. After I told him that, he then told me that the girls at Virginia State were prettier than the ones at his school. I said, "Okay, bet!" And that was the fastest offer I've ever accepted in my life. I was now officially a Virginia State Trojan.

I chose sports management as my major because growing up, I loved sports. I played both AAU and BNBL basketball, and

69

I played for my high school during freshman year. Early on, I knew that making it to pro was not in my future because I rarely started, and I got the most playing time when my team was down or up by 30 points—it was clear I wasn't a major asset to the team. All of my friends had pro-like potential in basketball and football, We devised a plan where we could all hit the real world and work together. I told them I'd go to college and study sports management, so when they all made it to the big leagues, I could be their sports agent, and then we'd be able to get money together. However, only a few of them made it to college but either dropped out freshman year, some got murdered, some got thrown in prison, others had to take care of their families, or just saw importance elsewhere.

It was freshman move-in day, and my uncle dropped me off to campus, where we carried all of my belongings inside of Williams Hall, where I would be staying. Making back-and-forth trips from the car to my dorm, there was a slew of accents from the resident assistants to the incoming freshman to students just walking by outside. After moving in everything, it finally hit me, I'm a real college student. I knew the transition from Baltimore to Petersburg would be different, but I didn't know what to expect. All I knew was that there were people back home rooting for me, and I was hoping that this "college" experience would make something out of me, and if not, I'd be sure to make something out of it. Both of my parents were in prison at this time, and neither of them had made my high school graduation, nor seen me off to college. It was bittersweet because I reached to a place that neither of them had been before, and they couldn't be there.

Virginia State was a new world to me, but freshman week got me acquainted to what I could expect of this experience. Freshman week is a designated week filled with programming intended to prepare students for college life. Everything from orientations, parties, and various other activities so students could get acquainted with one another and learn how to maneuver the yard. Some students even brought speakers out of their dorm rooms, placed them on University Avenue, and threw their own little parties. Freshman week was also the first time I learned that I have an "accent," and that because of it, people knew I was from either two places, Baltimore or London. Nearly everyone I encountered stopped midconversation to ask, "Where you from? Baltimore?" or "You from London? Your family from London?" They were intrigued by my distinct pronunciation of words like: blue, you, to, do, etc., where they claimed I made a funny "ewww," sound while saying the words.

After a few weeks into my freshman year, there was something at the forefront of my mind that I couldn't figure out. "What does HBCU stand for?" I kept seeing the acronym on clothes, poster boards; people were chanting "I LOVE MY HBCU" at sporting functions or just randomly on the yard. Hearing and seeing HBCU was very similar to my first time seeing the acronyms for "lol" and "lmao." When I saw people engaging with them on Twitter and Facebook years ago, I didn't know how to sound them out, didn't know what they meant, how they were used, and I didn't want to look like the oddball asking publicly, because as someone who chases the Internet, I should be hip to things like this. I had the idea that I'd just wait for the meanings to come into my life, or be vigilant when someone else asks, and see the response. But with HBCU, I needed to know, so I called my cousin Avon. Although he was at another school, he was still a source for my frequently asked questions, as he's always been.

"Yo, what's good A?"

"Nothing much, what's up?"

"Yo, what is an HBCU?"

There was a long dramatic pause. I thought he had hung up on me.

"Hello, hello? yoooooo"

"You dead serious?" he said with annoyance

"Yea yo, I'm serious."

"An HBCU is a historically Black college or university, dumbass."

My response was, "Ohhhhhhh, that's why there's no White people here!?"

And then Avon burst out laughing, and I joined in as we both made a mockery of my ignorance. At this point in my life, I had never watched movies like *School Daze*, or TV shows like *A Different World*, and *College Hill*, which shot one of their episodes at Virginia State. They all explicitly explored the dynamics of Black college life, and it was the core reason some chose to attend HBCUs.

HBCUs were established simply because of the racist ideas and policies that prohibited Black students from attending the traditionally White institutions. Structured higher education systems for Black people were nonexistent, which hindered us from countless job opportunities where you need certifications and degrees in order to apply. History was made when The Institute for Colored Youth, the first higher education institution for Black people, was founded in Cheyney, Pennsylvania, in 1837 and was later renamed the Cheyney University that we know today. It was followed by three other Black institutions: University of the District of Columbia, which was founded as a school for Black girls in 1851; then Lincoln University, in Pennsylvania in 1854; and Wilberforce University, in Ohio in 1856.

Learning what an HBCU was as a freshman, and all of the

rich academia-related history behind it, didn't stop me from getting lost in the social life—from the basketball and football games, to the beautiful Woo-Woo cheerleaders, to the fraternity and sorority parties, to "Fried Chicken Wednesday," to the midnight breakfast functions, and hanging in front of Foster Hall, and catching the party bus to the club in Richmond on the weekends.

After a few months of fun and getting adjusted to the college life, reality started to kick in. It was finally hitting me that being homesick was a real thing. For an extended period of time, I didn't hang out, or communicate with anyone frequently besides my grandmother through phone and text conversations, and with my girlfriend at the time. She was attending LIM College in New York, focusing on the business of fashion. I'd regularly catch the bus to NY, or she'd catch it down to where I was. Also, I found the simplest reasons to go back home to Baltimore to hang out with my friends. As I hung out on the block and roamed the streets in my Virginia State gear, everyone from gangbangers to churchgoers congratulated me for "making it out." I understood that the joy exuding from my community was because of the rarity of young Black men going off to four-year universities; however, the homesickness and pressures of spearheading a legacy were frustrating. Everyone expecting me to break generational curses, and to find my niche, and to make tons of money because that's what we're told college graduates do. All while I'm studying a major that's uninteresting, which was leading me to question, should I drop out?

With the guidance of my English professor Arnold Westbrook, I was able to start a life-changing journey. Professor Westbrook was unlike any other instructor I've ever had in my life. He channeled his English lessons through African American literature, which exposed me to Maya Angelou, Langston

Hughes, and other Black artists from music to film. In class we read and analyzed essays and documentaries like *Good Hair* by Chris Rock, we watched episodes of the *Boondocks*, and read rap lyrics. Until my encounter with Professor Westbrook, I never even knew the intricacies of rap music, and how the young and criticized genre is just as important as any other art form. All in all, I was falling in love with reading. I would skip some of my other classes just to sit in my dorm room and read everything from the dictionary to my favorite songs, and new books I grabbed from the university's library. Inhaling language and music, and learning new words, became a part of me. One day it had hit me . . . I never hated reading in grade school, I hated what my teachers were forcing me to read, and the way they tried to engage me in literature was ineffective.

One day, feeling inspired by Black artists, I decided to try out with poetry. I shared some of my poetry with a few loved ones, and they told me it was some of the best poetry they've ever read. My moment of excitement was cut short once I thought to myself, what if they are telling me that they like my work to spare my feelings? Or if I was a horrible poet, would they have told me? How much poetry do they read or listen to in order to know how to measure what "good" is? These were some questions that I asked myself. I decided to do something slick—I shared poetry with them that I had written but lied and told them it was by someone else. I'd read my friends the poem and say, "uh, yeah, this poem is by James Winkleberry III . . . he's from the north side of South Dakota, his favorite ice cream is butter pecan, and his favorite artist is Lady Gaga. And then I'd read them the poem, and they loved it, and my confidence began to grow again.

I hated my sports management courses and was falling asleep in almost all of my classes, because reading, and writing poetry was getting all of my attention. Sophomore year rolled around, and I was a part of a mentoring organization whose mission was to mentor first- and second-semester freshmen. My organization was having an upcoming Valentine's Day theme event, and the dance organizer who was scheduled to do our intermission backed out at the last minute. In my organization board meeting, discussing the event, I raised my hand and told them I'd perform a spoken word poem. With the exception of the few friends I shared my poetry with, no one else knew that I was writing. My organization didn't have anything to lose, so they gave me the green light.

February 10, 2013, was the day that changed my life forever. This was my first time performing in front of a crowd, and it was beyond scary. On top of the anxiety someone would traditionally face doing something public for the first time, rumor has it that the Virginia State student body booed the pop star Chris Brown when he performed at our university. In my mind, I kept wondering, if they booed Chris Brown, then what would they do to me if they don't like my performance? I went back and forth between the bathroom and Harris Hall, where the event was located. Several emotions were channeling through my body. I was nauseated, nervous, lightheaded, and excited all at once. Intermission rolled around, I was called to the stage, and after I performed my poem "True Love," the crowd erupted with claps. In that moment, still on stage, I told myself that I need to pursue my passion of poetry, and to do it by any means. The next day, I marched to Gandy Hall and switched my major to English, which was one of my most transformative decisions that I'd ever made in my life to that point.

I went from the quiet Baltimore kid to a well-known poet on campus. It started out as me performing at events on campus and holding my own unofficial open mic nights, to stretching outside to local open mics in Richmond. My personal growth fueled my desire to challenge myself and reach new heights. I then became Mr. Alpha Eta, where I served as the male figurehead for the Alpha Eta Chapter of Delta Sigma Theta Sorority Incorporated for two years. I was affiliated and respected amongst the English Honor Society, I became Mr. Senior, and I pledged the Nu Psi chapter of Omega Psi Phi Fraternity Incorporated, where I gained some lifelong brotherhood.

Virginia State University aided my personal development, as an artist, person, and the way they intellectually, spiritually, and emotionally equipped me for the world as I must face it as a young Black man. What Virginia State did for me is what HBCUs offer to young Black students who seek higher education in spaces that values Blackness. HBCUs are filled with promise and possibility, and the community that exists at these institutions has the ability to help Black students find beautiful pieces of themselves that they didn't know existed before attending an HBCU. Knowing or unknowingly, every day is a learning experience at an HBCU, inside and outside of the classroom. Just like any other university, Virginia State has its flaws, but when it all boils down, I love everything my HBCU did for me.

Imagine if I had a Black instructor like Professor Arnold Westbrook in grade school? What if I had had an instructor who used Black literature and modern strategies to engage me in literacy? Imagine if city schools gave students more space to be free within themselves, and the classroom? Maybe I would've found my love for literacy earlier on in life.

The call to consciousness here is to support HBCUs the best way that you know how, on any level. For instance, Makur Maker, a five-star basketball high school recruit, committed to attend and play for Howard University, a HBCU located in Washington DC. Traditionally five-star athletes don't attend HBCUs, or turn down offers to attend UCLA, Kentucky, Memphis, and other big-name sports programs, but that's exactly what Maker did with his decision to become a Howard Bison. Maker's announcement to commit to the HBCU was covered by *Good Morning America* to Fox News and was buzzing in the Twitter world, highlighting HBCUs across the country—and informing those like my old self of what an HBCU is. Hopefully Maker's decision will be the start of a movement that will urge young Black high school talent to attend and play sports for HBCUs, and bring more notoriety and money, and will help enhance the HBCU experience overall.

Beyoncé, one of the most influential artists today, paid tribute to HBCUs in her documentary *Homecoming* in 2019. Beyoncé never attended a Black university but said, "I always dreamed of going to an HBCU," which influenced her when creating the documentary. When *Homecoming* was first released, it sparked a worldwide conversation among those who never heard of HBCUs, and a celebration for us who are a part of the culture.

If you care about Black higher education, and it's within your means, find ways you can donate to HBCUs or official fraternities, sororities, and social organizations that exist on their campuses.

Some of my Black sisters and brothers will never step foot on a HBCU campus, but instead, a predominantly White institution (PWI), where they should be afforded the right and space to exist in their Blackness unapologetically. Are we creating, supporting, and maintaining these safe spaces for Black students at PWIs? How are you supporting their Black Student Union, if they have one? If I chose to attend Virginia Commonwealth instead of Virginia State, would I have had support from my institution and student body? Would they have the resources and bandwidth to support me?

Racist ideas are behind the belief that HBCUs are

inadequate, which then fuels racist decision making in policy, such as by Maryland Governor Larry Hogan, who on May 7, 2020, vetoed a bill that would have given the HBCUs in the state roughly $580 million by the year 2031. Antiracist thinking, on the other hand, is knowing that HBCUs are a piece of American culture that is progressive and have always been there to educate, uplift, promote, and maintain Black culture that was created by Black people. HBCUs are a result of what America denies Black people in this country. HBCUs are a symbol of hope for Black Americans—a symbol that reflects what we can achieve if we work together.

Tweets Aren't Loading Right Now

One of the popular things for people to do on the Internet nowadays is to dig up old tweets and showcase to the world how problematic a person once was, or which problematic ideas the person consumed in the past, and band together to get people to cancel them. It usually goes like this: a Twitter user will tweet something, and someone else will have in their possession an old tweet of that user, and will retweet their contradictory current tweet with that old one, alongside the caption, "This You?" Insinuating there's no way the user can't truly believe or stand on what they just tweeted, because of their past views. Some of these instances end up on what I call the new Summer Jam Screen, "The Shaderoom," an Instagram page that's known for stirring up controversy, posting celebrity gossip the majority of the time. Sometimes, people delete their tweets in the midst of controversy, so if someone clicks on the tweet it will say, "This tweet is unavailable," "Tweets aren't loading right now," "Tweet was deleted by author," and sometimes when the backlash is unbearable, when trying to click on the page, it will say, "Sorry, that page doesn't exist," indicating the author of the tweet deleted their Twitter account. When things like this occur, I always wonder, who is and who is not afforded the luxury to grow and learn from their mistakes?

I'm a part of Black Twitter, an online subculture dominated by Black Twitter users, where the content is endless. In Black Twitter, you can find people having discourse about community, you can learn new food recipes, or see guys arguing with their baby's mother. One day, I was scrolling through Twitter in late June and saw #CancelJemele trending on my timeline. Jemele Hill, former ESPN analyst, tweeted in 2009, "My FB friends are calling him 'Manny the Tranny' . . . so inappropriate and hilarious," calling former MLB star Manny Ramirez a "tranny" after he tested for the woman's fertility drug, gonadotropin. Many Twitter users from various communities were furious and called out Jemele's tweets as "transphobic."

Jemele addressed the tweet after the online backlash, "It was wholly ignorant, dumb, and offensive. I am ashamed that I was so uneducated about trans issues at the time. I stand with this community firmly today. I kept the tweet up because I welcomed the opportunity to apologize and to show growth . . . I care about the trans community I belittled and offended. If they don't see me as an ally because of this, it's my job to show them that I am."

Formerly known as "Noname Gypsy," the Chicago rapper decided to drop the "Gypsy" from her name in 2016. Noname tweeted, "I wanted to wait until my website domain name was changed but it is important for me to say this. I am no longer using gypsy in my name." She added: "When I first decided what my stage name would be, I was unaware of how racially inappropriate and offensive it was to Romani people. It was never my intent to harm or offend anyone in any way. That is not what I'm about. I'm sorry for any pain I previously caused. Please from now on address me as Noname :)" Recently she tweeted a list of "awful" mistakes she made, mentioning having "Gypsy" in her stage name, "saying that capitalism wasn't evil," and "performing in Israel instead of being in Palestine for the struggle for liberation," and ended off the tweet with "let this be a reminder that growth is an embarrassing but necessary process."

In 2019 Canadian singer Daniel Caesar was on Instagram Live defending his White friend Yes Julz against claims that she appropriates Black culture. "Being a victim doesn't get you paid . . . are there Black people in this chat right now?" Caesar asked. "Why are we being so mean to Julz? . . . Why are we being so mean to White people right now? . . . . White people have been mean to us in the past. What are you gonna do about that? Tell me what you're gonna do about that? There's no answer other than creating understanding and keeping it moving. You have to bridge the gap . . . Are we winning right now as a culture? Are we popular in society? We're not. And you can't win the game by choosing to not accept the winning team's strategy." In this rant, Caesar urged his fans to "cancel" him and not listen to his music. Later in the week, Caesar issued an apology: "I apologize for how I expressed my idea because that is where I went wrong. I believe in what I said and as a man, I need to admit when I am wrong. I can admit when I am wrong." He also called his rant tyrannical because he didn't have people around checking him, and he and his friends feel so strongly about what was said in his rant. However, he says he didn't realize how hard he was coming off, nor how he didn't leave room for dissent.

One thing that Jamele Hill, Noname, and Daniel Caesar have in common is that they publicly spewed language that harmed people due to their ignorance. However, they also elevated past that ignorance and righted their wrongs by issuing apologies, and claimed they've been actively working toward being more conscientious of how they voice their opinions on public platforms. Noname went so far as to start the Noname Book Club, who's mission is to uplift People of Color voices.

I too, spoke out of ignorance many times in my life, and I have an example of it on record.

In 2015, after graduating from Virginia State University with my BA in English, I didn't have my life path figured out, so I put all of my time and energy into my poetry, when I wasn't working as a pool attendant at Patterson Park. Aside from making me laugh at funny memes and engaging with my friends, Twitter serves as a daily news source for me. One day, I was scrolling Twitter and saw that Baltimore reached approximately 119 homicides for the year, and we were only halfway through the year at that point. News reports predicted that Baltimore was on track to have one of the deadliest years to date. Losing friends to violence has been routine for me since I was ten years old, and I'm not sure what it was about this exact moment, but I felt compelled to write about it, which came out in a poem titled "The Baltimore Bullet Train," which I shot a video for and released on YouTube. The poem was an emotional response to my feelings on gun violence in Baltimore. The video starts out with me hanging on the corner with a few of my homies, as the sliding doors of a minivan approached us, and guys started firing shots from inside. Then I was lying in the street, dead, and there was a circle of bystanders surrounding my lifeless, bloody body in disbelief. There's one scene where I'm arguing with my grandmother because I go against her wishes of not wanting me to hang out in the streets because it's "dangerous." And other small scenes that show clips of a graveyard, someone robbed at gun point, the agony people suffer when a loved one gets killed, among other things (full video on YouTube).

"The Baltimore Bullet Train" started to pick up steam, and I found myself being requested to perform the poem and sit on panels to speak on the issues around gun violence. I found myself at churches and funerals reciting this poem. The first was at The Empowerment Temple, at the funeral of a popular motorcycle rider who was murdered. And in June of 2016, popular Baltimore rapper "Lor Scoota" was murdered after leaving a charity basketball game—I recited the poem at his viewing and community appreciation service. If Scoota wasn't your favorite rapper, you respected his craft and, most important, his influence on Baltimore's music culture.

After every occasion where I performed this poem, I was bombarded with questions that I never fully had the answers to. "How do you feel about "Black-on-Black crime?" Or, "How do we stop the violence?" Or, "Why don't Black people care when they murder their own, and only care about police killings?" To name a few. As if we don't inscribe ink into our flesh after our loved ones are slain. As if we don't risk our lives and freedom to retaliate against the oppositions who killed our loved ones. As if Revenge ain't sweet, as if we don't crave it. We care so much so that parents go into debt to bury a body they used to pray for.

One of the lines in "The Baltimore Bullet Train" was "Congratulations, come on you gotta love it . . . isn't that what y'all do for fun? Measure the strength of a real man by who has less bullets in his gun . . . I mean who really cares about our people, apparently not us?" This was insinuating that people in my community are murdering for sport and receive immense joy from murdering.

I saw firsthand how gun violence mentally, spiritually, emotionally, physically, and financially ruins entire households, and still, my experiences alone could not fully address the issues I was dealing with in a way that humanizes my people. There's a saying, "standing too close to an elephant," which means you don't see the entire elephant, because your proximity to the elephant is intimate. Once I backed up from the elephant, I had some realizations.

I learned that speaking about the violence going on in my community, and others like it, was dangerous, because I was consuming racist and classist ideas unknowingly, and not addressing how the violence is clearly a symptom of systemic oppression. I was speaking out of ignorance from not deeply analyzing all that was happening all around me.

"The Baltimore Bullet Train" reflected my honest feelings at the time; however, I didn't address how the violence in my community is directly translated to the inferior circumstances we were confined to. I insinuated that there are "bad neighborhoods" out there in the world, when "bad neighborhoods" don't exist. There are neighborhoods that are underfunded; there are neighborhoods that are heavily policed; there are neighborhoods that have a long history of state-sponsored discrimination. The "good" neighborhoods are protected and overly funded by the state, and are policed less, which means that the people in those neighborhoods get arrested for fewer crimes but do not actually commit fewer crimes.

In the 1990s, Blacks were much more likely than Whites to be arrested and sent to prison because of racial biases. This fooled the masses into believing that since more homicides went down in Black neighborhoods, it automatically meant that Black people were using and dealing more drugs, among committing other crimes. As often as the violence in Black communities is catapulted in mainstream media—imagine if we showcased White violence and Whites committing crime? But since this doesn't happen, there becomes a fixed image in people's minds that Black inner-city neighborhoods are dangerous, poor Black people are animals, and therefore, they should be heavily policed and controlled in order for this country to be "safe" from crime. I've had a few friends whom I've met in college who thought about moving to Baltimore, and while they were searching for homes they'd ask me, "Is this a bad neighborhood?" or say things like, "I don't want to live in a dangerous neighborhood." I, too, was a person who used "bad" and "dangerous" to categorize neighborhoods, because that's what I was conditioned to say. That's what I was conditioned to believe—Black neighborhoods are bad and dangerous, and the White neighborhoods are safe. The "Dangerous Black Neighborhood" conception is based on racist ideas, and not reality. When you use words like "bad" and "dangerous" to categorize a neighborhood, knowingly or unknowingly, you are insinuating that that neighborhood is filled with bad and dangerous people. Anyone can consume and produce these ideas, even people who prove themselves to be pillars in their community by doing charity work.

"Gille Da Kid," a Philadelphia rapper and podcast host of "Million Dollaz Worth of Game," was recently dragged in the media for a video that resurfaced from four years ago, speaking on Black Lives Matter. In the video Gillie said, "All lives matter nigga . . . my life didn't matter to the nigga who tried to execute me . . . to the nigga that shot me in my muthafuckin wrist, stomach and foot." After the backlash Gillie said that he woke up to several texts in regard to the four-year-old video, which prompted him to make another one to clarify himself. He started off by saying, "Black lives matter, I support y'all . . . I support everyone that's on ground zero . . ." Gillie then noted he gave out turkeys to the community on Thanksgiving and passed out $30,000 worth of toys on Christmas: "Black lives is gonna matter, when it matter to Black people . . . if Black lives gon matter, that shit gotta matter all the time, not just when it's some injustices being done to us . . . but at the end of the fuckin day, if Black lives is gonna truly matter, it gotta matter with Black fuckin people . . ."

Does Gillie give back to his community and have a love for Black people? Of course, he does. However, he consumes and produces the racist idea that there is something wrong with Black people, who are to blame for the intercommunal violence, and not blaming the inferior circumstances that many Black people are padlocked to. Gillie doesn't understand that intercommunal violence in the Black community is in fact an injustice, and it directly correlates to the racist ideas and policies that are the heartbeat of this country.

Knowingly or unknowingly, most of us did, or currently do, consume the racist idea of the "dangerous Black neighborhood," and the "safe White neighborhood." We are conditioned to blame poor Black people, and not the system that oppresses them.

Are there dangerous neighborhoods out there that can be called "unemployed neighborhoods," "underfunded neighborhoods," "zero opportunity neighborhoods," "health service deprived neighborhoods," "hope deprived neighborhoods"? Absolutely. Ibram X. Kendi noted, "One study, for example, based on the national Longitudinal Youth survey data collected from 1976 to 1989, found that young Black males were far more likely than young White males to engage in serious violent crime. But when the researchers compared only employed young males, the racial differences in violent behavior disappeared."[1] Kendi goes on to explain that in Black neighborhoods, where unemployed people are concentrated, certain violent crime rates are elevated. He directly correlates this lack of opportunity, unemployment,

---

1   Kendi, Ibram X. *Stamped from the Beginning*, 436.

and other such factors as root causes to the violence in these Black communities.

It's America's duty to shift the blame onto the oppressed, and not the oppressors. It is their duty to create false racist scapegoats to ensure the idea of Black inferiority, and not ensure that we're knowledgeable about the laws, policies, and movements that keep us chained to discrimination.

Delores Tucker, a Black woman who was formerly in politics, declared war on rap music in the nineties, creating a strong campaign to dismantle the distribution of gangsta rap. In a nutshell, she believed that rap music is what made White people hold racist ideas about us. She believed that the lyrics in rap music were harming the Black community as a whole and that it was making us more violent, sexist, criminal, and materialistic. If gangsta rap was making Black listeners inferior, then what about the 80 percent of rap listeners who are White? When discussing how gangsta rap music negatively impacts Black people, why is it never brought up how the lyrics make White listeners more violent, sexual, criminal and materialistic?

For those who blame the forty-seven-year-old genre of music for plaguing the Black community, my homeboy Tariq Toure shared a series of tweets that we all should sit and think about: "If trap music creates violence what was King Leopold and Christopher Columbus listening to?" Another one was "If music is to blame then maybe Columbus was listening to 'Genocide or Die Trying,'" a lyrical play off of 50 Cent's debut studio album titled *Get Rich or Die Tryin'*. I understand the power of music as an influential force; however, creating a national campaign to blame rap music for the oppression of Black people is a convenience that neglects the long history of ill-treatment. The violence and criminality that are depicted in some, not all of the rap songs, are nothing but reflections of the world that we live in.

The moral of the story is that we all need time to grow. That is not to say that we shouldn't hold people accountable for their actions, but we must allow them the space to learn. Normally, when someone learns something new, they share it with others, especially if they are passionate about it. Just as I did with "The Baltimore Bullet Train," I identified an issue, gun violence, that was affecting me, and because I felt that I had a platform, I chose to speak about this issue because I was passionate about it. My words came from a place of love. As I continued to read more about antiracism, and intercommunal gun violence, I realized, "Whoa, I've been going on about this wrong." So now, I have to address the nature of communities with high unemployment rates and other racial disparities when I speak about the violence.

We have to remember that Malcolm X was Detroit Red— the hustler, dope boy, gambler, and pimp—before he become an activist and minister. We have to remember that Malcom X the activist minister, whom we romanticize for his "the White man is the devil" spill early on in his activism work, is the same man who had different views on that idea closer to his death. Malcolm X was having a discussion with an ambassador on one of his international trips and said to him, "What you are telling me is that it isn't the American White man who is a racist, but the American political, economic, and social atmosphere that automatically nourishes a racist psychology in the White man."

Malcolm X needed to be nourished and mentored by the Nation of Islam, in order to embark on his antiracism journey. Malcolm X needed time to grow, learn, and unlearn to understand the falsehoods in some of his teaching.

As we learn from our racist remarks and mistakes, it should be our duty to create spaces for other individuals to voice their thoughts, questions, and even ignorance, and to be honest about how they feel about race relations in this country. We need to be open and inviting to these people, so that they can become stronger in their antiracism work, and let them know that it is okay to be wrong, while also letting them know that "apologies" aren't the cure, but the work that one does is. I believe that if we create spaces like these, then people will be more open to speak about their current views, assumptions, and racist ideas, and we, who grew from our own ignorant racist remarks, can help others move one step closer to becoming antiracist.

Cool Tuesdays

Cheese-flavored sunflower seeds, two glazed honey buns, a bag of hot Cheetos, and a Huggie juice used to be the fuel that started my mornings. When I had an appetite midday, I'd contemplate eating a chicken box, a cheese steak sub, oily Chinese food, a burger, or pizza. And then, I'd choose one of the other items for my late night. Back in grade school, we were being fed poison—every meal less nutritious and more chemical-laden than the one before it. At home, fresh fruits and vegetables were subject to availability from local stores that overstocked processed goods often past their "sell by" or "use by" dates, so greasy, oily, or fried was the normal fare.

I was an adult when I first found out what a food desert was—and that I grew up in and was still living in one—and the dangers of it. Food deserts are generally defined as areas (mostly urban) with limited access to affordable, nutritious, high-quality, fresh food. It's common to see people in my neighborhood with amputated legs, arms, and toes after developing diabetes from unhealthy eating habits. I know several people who died or had near-death experiences from complications related to high blood pressure. Placing the blame on the people who live in impoverished communities, and not on the housing laws and regulations that shaped these environments into food deserts, is the common default.

Anthony Williams, comedian from Baltimore who goes by the name Cool Ant, is a good friend of mine, and he has a passion for outreach, which is reflected in the work he does in his community. He uses his 66,000 Instagram followers to help propel his awareness to issues that he believes should be actively worked on. Cool Ant's most recent venture, a nonprofit called "Neighborhood Hero," was inspired by Nipsey Hussle's nickname "Neighborhood Nip," the Compton Grammy-nominated rapper who was hailed for his community activism—but who we lost to gun violence on March 31, 2019. Cool Ant said that he wanted a new approach to engage with the community during the coronavirus pandemic, after learning that members of the Black community had an increased risk of getting Covid-19 or experiencing severe illness from the virus. "That's a whole different war we should be fighting," says Cool Ant. "It showed the life expectancy broken down by the zip code, and of course, the majority of Black neighborhoods had the worst."

With the help of some other community members, Cool Ant started a run club, which has now taken on the name "Cool Tuesdays," where people meet up every Tuesday at 6:00 p.m. to run, while also providing healthy, free food with the hopes of motivating people in their individual lives to continue a healthy lifestyle—something that I and many others were never taught while coming up. He funds the run club from donations that help him purchase healthy food and water. His run club has been growing weekly—with people traveling to Baltimore City from surrounding counties, and even from outside the state of Maryland, to attend the run. The spirit of this run club birthed a fitness group called "Building Bodies and Bonds," which focuses on various forms of exercise, while also building strong relationships with others to promote unity.

Systemic health and social inequities have long affected Black communities, so it's not a surprise that tracking data reveal that hot spots for the coronavirus are located in predominantly low-income Black neighborhoods. Severe illness and death rates are higher for racial and ethnic minority populations during public health emergencies than for other populations.

The plight of this current pandemic is one of many ways structural poverty impacts the Black community. Where you live in America determines whether or not you die—and the rate Black people are disproportionately dying is one of many examples. That's why it's blasphemous when racists say things like "racism will go away if we stop talking about it."

The racist will blame oppressed people for the horrific conditions they live in, and for their lack of healthy eating habits, but not blame the people who are actually in charge of making conscious policy decisions that impact and perpetuate poor and underserved neighborhoods to remain as they are. The antiracist will not only research to understand why racial disparities in housing, food, and death exist, but will work toward mitigating the disparities and being supportive of individuals like Cool Ant.

Cool Ant is the perfect example of one who identifies an issue within a community—coming up with quantifiable goals and a strategy to meet those goals and providing a roadmap that leads to helping others live a healthier lifestyle, which is ultimately fighting against structural poverty.

A Death Note

If the sounds of gunshots were generated into song sales, Baltimore would've gone triple platinum every year. In August of 2017, there were more than 220 murders in my city. Just a month before, I remember it was 3:00 a.m. and I was laying down on a pint-sized mattress in a cramped dorm room at the University of Illinois in Chicago. I had had a long day of writing workshops, so I decided to hit up the The Violet Hour, a bar in Wicker Park, where I guzzled four vodka gimlets to end my late-night/early morning. I was plastered, numb to all misery, until my phone buzzed. I checked it, and the alert read, "Man killed in Greenmount Avenue shooting becomes city's 200th homicide victim." I stared at the ceiling as cold tears slid down my cheek, chilling the back of my neck. I started to reminisce about all of my family and friends who expired on the streets of Baltimore. Depression crept down on me, hope seemed futile, and I wanted to fade out like Robin Williams. I called on God, but his phone was on Do Not Disturb; it seems as though he always ignores me when I need him the most. Every time a body drops in my city, no matter if it's a loved one or not, a piece of my sanity is chipped away.

We live in a country that marks Black babies at a popular price of null and void. Since I was a small child, I've had family and friends murdered under these Baltimore skies, and it's been killing me.

It was the summer of 2003, when bullets snatched all twenty-six years of Trav's life. Trav was my Aunt Lisa's boyfriend, and my Uncle Neil's best friend. Trav treated me like I was one of his own, and the love was mutual. I was ten years old, and school had just ended for the year. I was chilling with Uncle Neil at his crib, waiting for him to get dressed, so we could go back around my way and meet up with Trav. I was wakened out of my sleep by a loud "Nooooooo, not my nigga!" This would be an introduction to a phrase that inevitably became commonplace as I grew older. His shriek suppressed the lyrics of 50 Cent's *Get Rich or Die Tryin'* that were blasting through the speakers. I woke up and saw Uncle Neil pacing back and forth throughout the living room while veins bulged out of his sweaty forehead. I was afraid to ask what was wrong. But my childlike curiosity burned. "Unc, what happened?" A minute or two passed, and he sat on the couch beside me and cried. I didn't know what was going on, but I felt his pain, and I started to cry, too.

"They killed Trav," Uncle Neil said, as he struggled to get the three words out. This was also my introduction to "they." "They" is a person or persons that I would also hear stories about for a lifetime.

Uncle Neil and I walked on Hillen Road and flagged down a hack, and were driven to my house, two blocks over from where Trav was murdered. When we arrived, the entire neighborhood was in shambles. I can't remember a soul who wasn't crying. For the next few weeks I witnessed how Trav's death tore Uncle Neil apart. The harsh smell of rotten teeth mixed with Steele Reserve

211 was rushing out of Uncle Neil's mouth every time he spoke. Liquor was his fling-turned-wife.

This is my earliest memory of being spiritually and emotionally connected to death in Baltimore, and also my first time seeing how it affected the people around me. However, this wasn't my last. My Aunt Lisa, on the other hand, has had three of her significant others slaughtered in my city. Because her chin is always parked in the air, she doesn't ever show the slightest glimpse of grief, but I'm sure she's afflicted with pain.

My second encounter with death was later that same year of Trav's farewell. This time, it wasn't a close friend, and it wasn't murder. It was my seven-year-old little brother Fidel and his eleven-year-old brother Davon. I wasn't familiar with the word "suicide," but I knew that I didn't want to live any longer, and I was coming up with all sorts of ways to make that happen.

After Trav, Fidel, and Davon all died in such a short time, I knew for sure that I was gonna bite the dust soon.

* * *

Keon was 16 years old when a bullet struck his dome while standing on an East Baltimore corner in 2009. I was 16 at the time, too. Hours before his brains splattered on dirty marble steps, Keon rode through my block to holla at me.

"Yo, Ima bring some girls through the block later, they bad as shit."

"Bet, just hit my phone, I'll be around," I responded, as I gave him a fist bump and watched him wheelie away on his silver Mongoose.

A few hours later, my homie Dre ran up Jefferson Street wearing a sweaty gray wife beater. In and out of deep breaths, Dre said, "Yo . . . Guess what? . . . Keon . . . Just got popped!" I dropped my iced tea, and my homies and I sprinted toward

Linwood Avenue, where Keon was hit. As soon as we arrived, the street was decorated with yellow tape, blue and red lights, and women in PJs, shaking their heads while tears drained from their ducts: a sight that became a day-to-day thing.

A white sheet covered a body, which I denied was Keon until I scanned the premises and saw his lone green 498 New Balance sneaker napping in the middle of the street. This was my first time seeing a visual representation of a popular phrase in conversation in my neighborhood, and in rap songs: "Blow a nigga out his shoes."

Where I come from, crying is a sign of weakness, so I routinely rubbed my eyes, making sure no tears fell.

Keon was gone, and all I kept asking myself was "Will I be next?" To hide this pain, I was freakin-off with a massive amount of women, I was barely eating, I drank Four Loko long after my bladder felt like it was gonna burst, and I smoked hella blunts. I had hopes of going to college, but I just knew that the streets would do me in before freshman orientation because everybody's melon was gettin' cracked. Death was all around me, and it didn't have an age limit or gender preference.

* * *

April 14th, 2014, I was sitting in Gateway Hall, a dormitory at Virginia State University. I was working on promotion material for a collection of poems I was planning to release. I received a call from my little brother Antuane. "Yo, Shad got stabbed." Shad was my best friend. We shared clothes, shoes, and money. Shad's grandmother sold weed, but she always gave us dimes for free. One night she gave us something close to an ounce, and we shared it with these two sisters from our neighborhood and ended up bangin' them both on the same bed. Shad was a friend that I'd give my last. My last kidney, my last shot of yak, my last piece of chicken, you name it.

I instantly hung up the phone with Antuane and started praying. I got another call from him ten minutes later, and I heard him crying through the other end. I screamed, "Don't do this to me, Tuane. Why the fuck are you lying?" He continued to cry, then he said, "Shad is gone, my nigga." I left out of the lounge area and started walking back to my room. My motor skills conked; you would've thought Mike Tyson punched me in the stomach the way I dropped to the floor. My tears flooded the floor, as people walked past, looking at me as if I were crazy. At this point, I wouldn't have disagreed with them. I was broken.

I went home and found out that Shad got into an altercation with a guy at a gas station. A fight broke out, and Shad got jabbed in his liver several times with a small sword. He crawled into his car and locked himself inside to escape the clutches of his newfound enemy. Shad's suede seats chugged liters of his blood, and he slithered into the opening arms of the grim reaper.

Y'all know what I did for the next few months: gave no fucks and went to class drunk damn near every day, as professors gave me side eyes. I know they smelled that sauce seeping through my pores.

Every day for the next few months, alcohol bit a hole in my pocket, and I routinely locked myself in my dorm room for many nights with 2 Pac's "Thugz Mansion" and Rihanna's "What's Love Without Tragedy?" on repeat, as I killed myself. They were the only two songs that could understand me. I got disconnected from many of my college friends because I inched further away from the guy they once knew.

I became careless and dispassionate when it came to school and relationships. I wanted to be by myself, and many people just couldn't understand. I thought that I was gonna drink myself into a casket or die from stress before I even made it to senior year. I was ready for the ride.

* * *

D was twenty-one when he got splashed in West Baltimore. It was January 2015.

I had just returned to my neighborhood after performing some spoken word poetry to a group of students. I was standing out front of JJ's carryout in East Baltimore, watching cars bounce down the lumpy roads of Monument Street as I waited for my chicken box. Fifteen minutes passed, and I walked into the store to check on my food. "Ayyeee Mama! Those 4-wings-and-fries ready?" I said as I tossed my ticket into the circular plexiglass portal where money, food, and arguments about wrong orders get exchanged. I received my food, left JJ's, and stopped inside of Rod's Barbershop, which is a few stores down. As I gave dap to friends and associates, I received a call.

"Yo guess what?"

"What's good?"

"You heard D got murked last night?"

I hung up my phone in disbelief and shrieked, "Fuck!" while everyone stared. I left the barbershop and did what I do best to cope. I hit the liquor store and grabbed a pint of Absolut and a pack of Black & Milds and started my healing ritual.

D, Shad, and I all hung in the same camp. Every time I looked at old pictures of me and my friends, I saw fewer people, and I couldn't help but to embrace an early death. I mean, how could I not?

Suffering from the mental and emotional pain that stems from murder and violence is one of the many ways that Black people die in America. Every single day I ask, "Will the murder ever stop?" and the more I learn, I understand the hard truth, and the answer is, no. Aside from the names of the people I mentioned above that died, there are countless deaths that troubled me while living in Baltimore and being connected to her hip. I have stacks of obituaries, and I can't count how many funerals I attended.

A list of things I've seen at funerals: fistfights amongst friends, family, and I've even seen a pastor get knocked out by a quick jab. Drunken fathers have jumped in the ground screaming, "I want to be buried with my son," at burial sites. I even know of some people who committed suicide after losing a loved one. When anger has been bottled up for ages, anything is liable to take place.

I can't count how many shoulders I cried on, nor the number of people I lent shoulders to.

Everyone in my city knows someone who's been murdered. Thousands of people are suffering from some type of mental anarchy that stems from violence. As I started to do research on violence and murder, the tragedies in Baltimore started to make sense.

* * *

I stumbled across an article in Bloomberg that said, "Baltimore is the worst place in America to grow up poor and male." I know that my city is extremely difficult to survive in, but I never knew that it was the worst in the country. I did more scholarly lurking and discovered that Harvard economists Raj Chetty and Nathaniel Hendren researched a child's chances of future success by collecting a list of the 100 largest counties in America.

The two economists' studies show that "Baltimore is at the bottom. But it's really at the bottom for boys." This is a result of what I call "zip code genocide."

Baltimore is a city where "everyone knows each other." This city has roughly 620,000 residents, and 63 percent of those people are Black. The Black people stay and hang out where they live, and vice versa for White people. Baltimore has two identities, and what you call it depends on where you reside. My friends and I grew up referring to it as "Bodymore Murderland."

The White people call it "Charm City." We eat chicken boxes and other phony foods while standing on small blocks adjacent to dice games under blue lights, and we converse about who got murdered the night before, the new chicks who moved in the hood, and who got beat up by the cops that day. We drink cheap vodka that burns our chest and temporarily scraps our heartache. White people walk their expensive dogs, do yoga, have avocado food fights in Whole Foods, and drink Non-GMO-Gluten-Free Pinot Grigio, I think.

Nonetheless, there are two Baltimores, and your zip code determines whether or not you live or die. Poor and concentrated communities have lower employment, lower educational attainments, higher crime, and poorer health outcomes than other areas. The History, Public Policy, and the Geography of Poverty data reveal, "About 80 percent of Baltimore City's poor live in a poverty area, whereas across the rest of the State, 17 percent of the poor live in a poverty area."[1]

Poverty is a modern-day slave ship with a little more leg room.

Poverty imprints barriers that deny Black people the opportunity to achieve promising education, well-paying jobs, and sanity, which leads to murder, depression, and suicide. Suicide doesn't always come with a rope, pistols, or prescription pills. In poor living circumstances, suicide is masked up in drug addiction, self-doubt, murder, and other things, which stifle Black progression and strengthen Black people's despair.

The large majority of Americans expect Black people to "pull themselves up by the bootstraps," and become "better

---

1   Botts, Jennifer, et al. "Understanding Challenges Facing Baltimore City and Maryland." Department of Legislative Services, January 2016, http://mgaleg.maryland.gov/pubs/budgetfiscal/2016-geography-of-poverty.pdf.

people," and that will amend poor Black people's economic status, and the racial disparities, and the racial discrimination they face. Placing these incriminations on Black people and not the systems that enslaves, murders, and oppresses Black people, is criminal. It is also one of the many racist ideas that keep Black people chained to an inferior status in this society.

* * *

If resources are not put into the underserved communities like the one I come from, poverty will remain undefeated, squeezing people into emergency rooms and graveyards. Grandmothers will outlive their grandkids, and the smell of sizzling flesh will dangle over nappy fades and colorful barrettes.

However, I'm supposed to pretend that I'm happy, while I walk on ground where shy blades of grass grow plump from swallowing the blood of babies.

I'm supposed to pretend that I'm happy, while I wait on bus stop corners where deflated balloons choke dirty light poles, and hard melted candle wax covers marble steps, the cries of mothers attending vigils ricocheting on my ear drums.

I'm supposed to pretend that I'm happy, although a million screams from absent sons and daughters ride my brain eternally. I'm supposed to pretend that I'm happy, while envisioning the faces of the crying children that killed you: the ones who pop pistols shed tears, too.

I'm supposed to pretend that I'm happy, knowing that death has said its farewell to "around the corner" and is now dancing at my peephole. I'm supposed to pretend that I'm happy, knowing that many parents don't have a fair chance at raising their children productively in this smoky city.

I'm supposed to pretend that our zip codes don't determine whether or not we live or die? I'm supposed to pretend that zip-code genocide doesn't lead to depression, suicide, and homicide? Nevertheless, I don't have any more patience in me to be fake-happy. I'm aching, my sanity has been shattered, and I don't mind accompanying the rest of them in paradise, if there is one.

There are more than 16,000 run-down vacant homes in my city, and we lose loved ones to murder and drug overdoses every day. Where I live, there are no "safe spaces." Where I live, yoga can't stop bullets from piercing through the livers of my homies. As long as there is poverty, there will be murder, and where I live, blood will continue to be shed.

Just like SZA, "I'm prayin that my 20 somethings don't kill me."

I don't have a one-size-fits-all solution to these problems, but I do have hope. I've explained in this book that mine has been an evolution of experience, realization, reflection, and profound desire to be a force for furthering the dialogue toward action. I try to highlight in this book some people and organizations that are doing their best to elevate the culture for positive impact and effective change.

Rest in peace to all of the children who were born—a bullet wound, a bad day, a bloody skull, a body bag.

As long as guns thunderclap, striking holes through flesh: so long live the lost Black angels, and the ones who are next. I hope that this song serenades forever.

Black Body as Temple

Sitting down and having a conversation with Sharayna Christmas made me view dance in a different light.

Christmas makes it clear that when she mentions the word "dance," body and movement are in the backseat, discipline of the mind is riding passenger, and spirituality is behind the wheel. Dance is a roadmap to become one with the raison d'être of the Black body, which Christmas believes are the ancestors that live within it. In 2003, she started Rayn Fall Dance Studio, a ballet school for Black children in Baltimore; however, it was never about just being a classically trained dancer. "I'm responsible for my people . . . dance is about how the body protects, communicates, and moves about; how it reacts to certain things," she says.

Black bodies that were once sold for crates of gunpowder and rum, bodies that America has always tried to reduce to things: how does one turn those Black bodies into temples used to educate Black youth with high-quality arts education?

Christmas's upbringing and journey address that head-on. Before it was a trend to care about Black bodies and the spaces that they occupy, the Harlem native was raised in a family where Black progression was at the forefront. Her mother was an Afrocentric community activist and member of the National Rainbow Coalition, the political organization founded by Jesse Jackson in 1984. She was an influential role model for her daughter, although, at ten years old, Christmas disliked being at marches, meetings, and mosques, because she was too young to understand the importance of the work her mother was doing.

In America, your zip code determines a lot: whether or not your schools look and operate like prisons; whether or not you get terrorized by police walking through food deserts to purchase everything GMO, and foods that can cause cancer; whether or not you die at an early age to gun violence; whether or not you have to fight for just "enough." There is no such thing as moral absolutism for the oppressed, because we don't play by the same rules as those who have or were born with "plenty"—a term that is understood as a paradise-only state. The rules that we have to break in half in order to survive in America will almost always reckon with the moral code of the "plenty holders." However, Christmas has no shame in telling us about the double-edged sword the Black body has to tote, in order to survive in America, while teaching your family its true history.

At a young age, she witnessed the unethical ways that Black bodies were being mistreated. "My past is not squeaky clean," she says. "If you have family 'like that' there's things you experience, that you'll be around that you can't help." Christmas grew up attending church regularly, but she had close family members who lived a life in the streets, which led them to incarceration, locking up the Black body. It was through personal accounts of having incarcerated family members, and mother-daughter trips to the NY Public Library's Schomburg Center for Research in Black Culture, where she recalls being educated about everything from the Haitian Revolution to literary giants such as Langston Hughes, whose work portrays the joy and suffering of Black lives during the early 1900s. The duality of her family awakened her revolutionary spirit.

"There were a lot of breakdowns . . . toxic things that happened; that was even my reason for coming to Baltimore," she says. "Although I came here for school, I wanted to build a livelihood that was outside of that. I came here and started to do the same things my mother did. Working with young people. Loving Black people." Christmas received her BA in Finance from Morgan State University in 2002, went back home to New York and took a job at Goldman Sachs, but returned to Baltimore in 2003 to teach Black youth ballet at the Druid Hill Park YMCA.

Christmas cites three dancers as her major influences, performers and artists who understood the value of the Black body. Alvin Ailey, the choreographer, activist, and founder of the Alvin Ailey American Dance Theatre in 1958 "saw the beauty in Black people and used dance to show us the way that they lived in the rural South," she says. She cites Arthur Mitchell, who used Dr. Martin Luther King, Jr.'s death as fuel to create a ballet school in the basement of The Church of the Master church, as the inspiration for her own creation of spaces for Black youth. "He knew that opening the school wasn't about him, so he is the person who influenced me the most," she explains. Pearl Primus, the dancer, choreographer, and anthropologist, resonates with Christmas as well, in her mission to uplift the reputation of African dance to American audiences.

Christmas started out wanting to provide Baltimore youth with opportunities to dance, so years later she created an organization called New Generation Scholars, where she teaches the youth about history through domestic and international travel. In the United States, her groups have been to New Orleans, New York, and nine international trips including Cuba, Jamaica, Costa Rica, Puerto Rico, the Dominican Republic, Haiti, the

Bahamas, London, and Paris. The group is scheduled to make their tenth visit in July of this year to Ghana.

Growing up in Baltimore, my friends and I knew that we had talent; we knew that we were different from the norm, but we didn't have any outlets to claim the gifts we possessed. Hip hop was the most influential genre of music in my life, but the rest of world called it "devil music" and blamed it for the violence in my community. When I was young, my friends and I loved to paint on our tennis shoes and alter our shirts, caps, and jeans with scissors, needles, and thread. The rest of the world said it was the way "thugs," "hoodlums," and "ghetto" people dressed, dehumanizing and criminalizing our culture, while we saw it as style. With music and fashion being the two forms of art that I had a love for growing up, I still always viewed them as "less than." We would have died for someone like Sharayna Christmas to see the genius in us and channel it through education and travel outside of Baltimore.

For Christmas, it's not enough to simply educate Baltimore youth; she wants to inspire them completely and physically through travel, in order for them to view their social context from a new perspective, both to recognize the value in their own lives and to realize there is a much larger world beyond what they were raised with. "Traveling outside of the United States is spiritual for me," she explains. "All locations are chosen to seek people that represent the African Diaspora throughout the world and through colonialism. When I take the young kids out of the country it refills them. They become better artists, curators, writers, and so on." After the immersive travel experiences, full of performances, visits to museums, and furthering their studies of the African Diaspora, her students are more prepared to set long-term goals for the future and make an impact with their work back in Baltimore.

"I feel like Baltimore really raised me, in a sense, to be the adult that I am," Christmas says. "I would never be like this in New York. I might've been an activist, but I wouldn't have a dance school, or I wouldn't be mentoring youth. I wouldn't have much of a presence and impact. Baltimore forces you to make sh*t happen. Black bodies in Baltimore are the epicenter of Black progression."

Christmas believes that when Baltimore improves culturally, economically, and socially, the lives of city residents will get better. She believes that Baltimore is a barometer for cultural progress: that the quality of life for Black people in Baltimore is a direct reflection of America's truth. She sees herself as part of the city's slow progression, through the power of art, culture, and education. "Baltimore has some of the most creative individuals I have ever met in my life," she says. "But, Black bodies in Baltimore are dying because the system is not done pimpin' Baltimore. They are not done using Baltimore as a poverty story."

Christmas is realistic about the challenges ahead of her, both personal and for the youth she works with, but her passion drives her to keep moving forward and to continue to offer opportunities for empowerment for Black bodies in Baltimore.

"Even though I accomplished a lot, I've got a lot of healing to do," she admits. "I'm responsible to my people. Now what does that cost me? It costs me a lot: mentally, spiritually, physically. If I had it my way, right now, I'd rather be somewhere in somebody's village, with somebody's grandmother, giving me the space to just experience the sun. Because of all the work that we do, sometimes we just need a second to heal and refuel ourselves. And I feel like that can only happen on the continent, in Senegal."

It's Always 12 O'Clock

In Baltimore, dirt bike riding is spiritual and is one of the major staples in our culture. I remember being a child, sitting in the living room watching TV, playing video games, eating, or just simply chilling, and the sound of dirt bikes made me run through the front door, and stand on the corner and watch the guys wheelie, and hit tricks up and down the block. The dirt bike group was called the "12 O'Clock Boys." They gave themselves that name because they can wheelie their bikes for miles with their front wheel aimed to the sky, sometime even scraping their back fenders on the concrete, which was an indicator that you were really having the bike at the 12:00 angle. If there were collectible trading cards featuring the riders, I'm pretty sure my friends and I would've all owned some as kids.

Dirt bike riding in Baltimore has been illegal for as long as I can remember. It's also illegal for the police to chase unauthorized vehicles. Throughout the years, police officers and dirt bike riders have either got severely injured, or died during chases, which prohibited the chasing. The state considers dirt bikes public safety risks, but not the cops? Not the government officials who allow the police to terrorize? Not the educational systems?

The state is more focused on the "potential hurt" of people instead of the real everyday hurt that is threatening Black lives.

Baltimore's police budget is $530 million dollars, and they've made the decision to build a Dirt Bike Task Force to "combat" dirt bikes, but regularly allows Arenacross riders to come to our city to ride at the Royal Farms Arena, the same "illegal" bikes that Baltimore residents get arrested and terrorized over. This city allowed Jada Pinket Smith and Will Smith, executive producers of the film *Charm City Kings*, to shoot for three months in Baltimore, while the actors and actresses rode dirt bikes through the city.

When the electronic scooter company Bird first hit our city, by law they were considered unregistered, illegal, until late 2019, when they got registered under the Maryland vehicle law. Instead of targeting illegal dirt bike riders, if the state truly cared about inner-city kids and their interests, they would be supporting Brittany Young and her organization, B-360.

Brittany Young, a Black woman from Baltimore, saw issues in the city revolving around dirt bike culture and decided to take matters into her own hands to help the situations. As a kid, Brittany was engaged in watching the dirt bike riders do stunts and fix and repair their own bikes. This is one of the reasons that inspired her to create solutions through B-360, a STEM education program that hires former street riders to teach the engineering design process, mechanics of dirt bikes, low-risk riding techniques, and allowing recreation in safe spaces.

Her programming calls out the need to lessen nonviolent crimes, specifically for riding dirt bikes, working to replace jail time and fines with community service, disrupting the school to prison pipeline. She uses her experience in STEM to create programs geared toward building bridges in communities, advocating for more relevant ways to teach STEM to children who live in low-income areas. She also works with other cities to create diversion programs, advocate for dirt bike spaces, and to cautiously showcase the style of riding that could draw cities and riders earned revenue.

Following the uprising of Freddie Gray in 2015, the conversation about jobs, opportunities, and resources for Baltimore youths was surfacing. The Associated Black Charities published a report showing Baltimore had over 120,000 midlevel STEM careers that did not require a four-year degree to move communities out of poverty.

Brittany knows that, if STEM is taught by telling someone to read a book instead of how it already relates to his or her everyday life, these careers can seem unattainable, so she channels it through dirt bikes

After the uprising is when Baltimore decided to start a Dirt Bike Police Task Force to uphold the law that criminalizes riders for possession of dirt bikes and for riding. Brittany agreed that people should be out of traffic but also wanted there to be programming and positive reinforcement to get to the same outcome and allowing choices. Since launching in 2017, B-360 has served over 7,000 students, hired 32 dirt bike riders, and worked to shift the culture. In 2019, she hosted three events in Texas, Baltimore, and Atlanta to showcase the riding style, and other cities are now interested in creating spaces for riders.

She believes the people closest to the problem should be utilized as assets for solutions. We need to fund the people, and B-360 is an example of what happens if funding can be placed in the hands of Black leaders to serve their own communities and work to strengthen their antiracism activities. Imagine what Baltimore would be like if we defunded the Baltimore Police Department and put those funds into organizations like B-360, which cares about the future and well-being of Black youth.

Brittany is the first person whom I've came across who saw the potential in dirt bike riders, viewing them as talented natural-born mechanical engineers and helping them develop their talent into STEM careers. Not only will the youth learn skills, but they are skills that can be passed down to others. I believe Brittany Young is the perfect example of how you can raise awareness to the importance of relatability in education from a real-life, situation and use her platform to help improve social innovation.

B-360 is now. B-360 is the future.

Baltimore Ceasefire 365

There is no one-size-fits-all solution to stop the violence, but there is a radical and ground-breaking movement happening in Baltimore to slow it down and revitalize how people cope with the trauma. PTSD is an unsung tune in our community, but it inflicts mental instabilities on the thousands of people in the aftershock of their loved ones being killed—Baltimore Ceasefire 365 is a blessing to all of us.

The goal is for people around the city to engage in life-affirming activities, along with putting a muzzle on violence in the community. The first cease-fire took place the first weekend in August of 2017, and there were no murders for a total of sixty-seven out of the seventy-two hours. This was still ground-breaking, as statistics proved—since at this time there was one murder every nineteen hours. The second cease-fire, which took place three months later in November, saw art installations, workshops, and a community tailgates but was marred by a murder twenty-six hours in. Some of the programming consisted of people leaving visible markers in the places where people have been killed—turning murder scenes into sacred ground.

Baltimore Ceasefire 365 was founded by a Black woman

named Erricka Bridgeford, with an organizing committee of five men and women from across the Baltimore community. Mrs. Bridgeford's own harrowing journey is behind the idea: murder snatched two of her cousins, a brother, and a stepson.

"Every time there's a cease-fire weekend and someone gets killed, we immediately find that family and give them money," explains Bridgeford. Funds are donated, and she goes to explain that the money can be used for anything from funeral expenses to fresh sneakers, noting that healing mechanisms are subjective and that they want what's best for everyone.

In the process of hitting the streets, Mrs. Bridgeford and other organizers ask the people of the community, "What do you need in your life that will help make things better for you and your loved ones?" The idea is to be hands-on, sharing resources that can help people struggling with legal issues, financial trouble, and mental health issues.

The Baltimore Ceasefire is geared not only toward stopping shootings, but all violence. I spoke with Hannah Brancato, who's a part of the Monument Quilt Project and who held a workshop during one of the cease-fire weekends to honor victims of domestic homicide. On the quilt were collections of stories from people who've been impacted by rape and abuse, along with messages of support from others.

I asked Brancato her thoughts on the importance of practicing art in communities—and specifically, the way in which yoga and fitness can be practiced in urban communities to help heal the people. Hannah responded, "Envisioning the world we want to live in, and dreaming about something different, is necessary for social change work—and for our own well-being. In that way, we can be free and help each other get free."

As I scanned the room, I saw Bridgeford's mother, who was sitting with her eighteen-year-old granddaughter. I asked them about generational trauma, since all three of them are engaged in working on a solution. Bridgeford's mother saw domestic violence as a child but believes the cycle stopped because she was able to limit what her children would and would not see. It was these principles that her daughter would carry forward when raising her own children.

Much like Mrs. Bridgeford and her family, I believe that if we can pass down trauma from generation to generation, we can do the same with healing and nurturing, forming new foundations of love. Baltimore Ceasefire 365 is showing us the way.

Slippin' into Darkness

Last year, I texted a friend and told her that I had a vivid dream she committed suicide. Loved ones were sharing pictures they took with her, and blogs were covering the story. She wasn't a close friend, so initially I felt conflicted whether I should tell her or not—didn't want her to be creeped out. Something in the universe told me to reach out to her, to check and see if she was doing well. I went ahead and shared a voice note through text which led to a phone call. She told me that she was not suicidal and was actually in one of the best spaces in life than she's ever been. I felt at ease until she told me something along the lines that dreams are real, but sometimes all of the characters in them are not who they appear to be, and encouraged me to check on the people closest to me, because they might be suicidal.

A week later, I got a call telling me that one of my childhood friends, who also attended elementary/middle school with me, had committed suicide. He was a scholar, entrepreneur, activist, and one of East Baltimore's very own. He was found hanging in his closet, along with a note written to his mother.

Suicidal thoughts were always common growing up. It was blasphemous to say it out loud; however, it was disguised in the music we listened to, and the lyrics we decided to post on our Myspace and Facebook pages. We could always go back and say, "it's just a song" if someone chose to question it. Black Americans face unprecedented stress, isolation, depression, and paranoia being oppressed in a place we are supposed to view as home. With the COVID-19 pandemic, there is an increase in unemployment and social isolation. Studies are showing that people are experiencing higher rates of anxiety, depression, and harmful drug use due to the stresses caused by coronavirus. Researchers at the Well Being Trust, a national foundation focused on mental wellness, and the Robert Graham Center, an independent research unit associated with the American Academy of Family Physicians, predicted that "alongside the thousands of deaths from COVID-19, the growing epidemic of 'deaths of despair' is increasing due to the pandemic—as many as 75,000 more people will die from drug or alcohol misuse and suicide."[1]

Every time there's some kind of national crisis, Black people in underserved communities get hit the hardest.

* * *

A scarred brown palm flew in the air. A squeaky preteen voice followed: "Can you tell me how to cope with suicidal thoughts? Because sometimes I just don't wanna be here anymore."

I was sitting in front of a class of middle-schoolers who were reading my book *Raw Wounds*, when a student asked this haunting question. I had asked the kids, "Do you have any

---

1 "The COVID Pandemic Could Lead to 75,000 Additional Deaths from Alcohol and Drug Misuse and Suicide." Well Being Trust, https://well -beingtrust.org/areas-of-focus/policy-and-advocacy/reports/projected -deaths-of-despair-during-covid-19/.

questions before I start speaking?" assuming that they would've asked questions about my book; however, I was wrong.

My tongue got replaced with a stone. My throat got clogged—it felt like a gun was jammed in the back of my mouth.

My mind scrambled like a quarterback in the pocket—it was fourth and long in the final quarter with seven seconds left on the clock, we were down by two points. I peeked through the bars on my face mask, head moving back and forth. I looked for an open receiver, BOOM! I'm sacked. I fumbled.

This wasn't the first time that a student asked me a question like this. However, because I didn't have a response, this particular altercation lit a fire inside of me.

Suicide is the sixteenth-leading cause of death for Blacks of all ages, and the third-leading cause of death for Black males between the ages of fifteen and twenty-four. After researching this information, I had a better understanding as to why children want to kill themselves. I live in a city where children are eyewitnesses to violence and murder. I live in a city where grandparents bury their children and grandchildren regularly. I live in a city where lead paint poisoning and fentanyl are snatching lives. I live in a city where your zip code determines whether or not you die. I live in a city where kids have knocked on God's door, been ignored several times, then come to me asking about suicide. Many of these children can't picture better lives for themselves—some will never get a crumb from that American pie that everyone tells us to strive toward—and killing themselves seems like the best option.

Suicide Awareness Voices of Education studies show that seven in 100,000 youth aged fifteen to nineteen die by suicide each year, and 12.7 in 100,000 young adults aged twenty to twenty-four die by suicide each year. Male deaths represent 79 percent of all US suicides, and there is one death by suicide in the US every twelve minutes.[2] There is so little conversation about so much bloodshed.

I came across a headline that read, "Family stunned by Boy's Suicide Attempt That Killed Driver." A twelve-year-old boy belly flopped from an overpass in Virginia and ended up landing on an SUV, killing a twenty-two-year-old woman."[3] I also found out that a ten-year-old boy stabbed himself in the chest, taking his own life in Memphis, Tennessee. These two incidents are deeply troubling; however, they are lint-ball-sized when you take a glimpse of the rate that young people are killing themselves.

In 2015, the Centers for Disease Control and Prevention discovered for the first time ever that "the suicide rate of Black children between the ages of five and eleven had doubled between 1993 and 2013. . . . Suicides by hanging nearly tripled among Black boys in particular."[4]

In impoverished communities similar to the one I am from and currently live in, suicide and depression are words that are always left out of conversation when speaking about the ways that Black people die. Being as these acts of suicide regarding Black people are directly connected to poverty and poor race relations in America, there is not a universal solution to this issue. What I will say is that we need to start being more open

---

2   Suicide Awareness Voices of Education, https://save.org/about-suicide /suicide-facts/.

3   "Woman Killed After 12-Year-Old Boy Jumps Off I-66 Overpass, Lands on Her SUV." NBC Washington, October 29, 2017, https://www.nbc -washington.com/news/local/police-suicide-attempt-by-boy-jumping -from-overpass-kills-driver-below/31331/.

4   Zielinski, Alex. "Why Are So Many Black Kids Dying From Suicide?" *Think Progress*, February 22, 2016, https://thinkprogress.org/why-are-so -many-black-kids-dying-from-suicide-6145b78764f6/.

about our feelings and emotions wholeheartedly, so we can shift the culture and the way that we handle discussions around suicide and depression.

We need to create spaces for people to be honest about their feelings, and what it is that they go through. Being open about what's killing you can help save a life or two. I know that working through and revealing my vulnerability in my work has helped me and others out.

Viral Executions

My execution might be televised
—Freddie Gibbs

It's hard for many of us to unglue our eyes from phone screens these days. Hourly digesting everything from funny memes, fights, cooking tutorials, to sports highlights, and clips from our favorite movies. Social media is a pile of images, videos, and words that allows us to see what people are thinking and doing, and it keeps us updated with the world's politics. And lately, dead Black bodies have been the main attraction to gain social media attention through retweets, shares, and comments. America does an excellent job at showing minorities their place in this country. It's hard for me to not think about the dead Black bodies that I see on my social media timeline, even after I log off—like a video of George Floyd crying for his dead mother, while the racist killer cop Derek Chauvin kept his knee on Floyd's neck for eight minutes, killing him and not breaking a sweat—the whole world saw it. Mike Brown's lifeless body planking on a Ferguson Street for four hours, after being murdered by the killer cop Darren Wilson. Baltimore police dragged Freddie Gray's limp body after beating him into a seven-day coma, where he later died—the whole world saw it. In a world where the terms "mental health," and "self-care," are more frequently mentioned on public platforms, I can't help but to think how these viral videos are affecting Black people psychologically. What do safe spaces look like for us, when we get constant reminders of what our public execution could potentially look like?

Being Black in America is having to wake up every day knowing there's a fixed image of you in the minds of the producers and consumers of racist ideas, and knowing that they can act on those images, and treat you accordingly. It doesn't matter if you have a LLC, college degrees, or if you drive the latest BMW—if you are Black in America, your freedom is threatened just by existing. Racist cops can murder you, and not get convicted of any charges, and will still be labeled heroes by the American people. The killers with badges will still be able to go on vacations with their families, get discounts on coffee and sandwiches from their favorite restaurants, and still keep their jobs. Being Black and conscious of how racism works is to constantly be in rage. Outside of what you personally deal with, being Black in this country and constantly seeing public displays of racism can take a toll on you mentally.

I was walking down Charles Street in the Station North Art District in Baltimore, and as I passed the Amtrak train station, a huge electronic billboard caught my eye. The billboard read, "George Floyd," with a scribbled heart over the top of it. My mood shifted, but I continued on my journey. A friend of mine put me on game to this app called Pattern and told me that it helps inspire consciousness and empathy through zodiac signs. I had recently downloaded the app, so I decided to check it out, with the hopes of getting lost in it, taking my mind off of the current state of the world. As soon as I opened it, there was a Black Lives Matter statement, addressing their support for victims of police brutality. I closed out my phone and stuffed it back in my pocket. I walked another block or so, pulled my phone out again, and attempted to listen to some music for a little therapy, and when I opened up Apple Music, there was a statement saying that they canceled their usual Beats 1 schedule and directed users to a single streaming station that celebrates what they call "the best in Black music." I shut out my app, logged onto Twitter, and all I was saw were videos of George Floyd being executed. And Black Twitter was advocating for the reopening of Breonna Taylor's case so that her death could be investigated, and with the hopes of her killers getting convicted of murder. Other tweets and videos of police brutality, racial injustices, and RIP posts for people who've died from gun violence also dominated. In minutes, my entire day was ruined, and it was all caused by the constant reminder of the price that we pay as Black people in this country.

Propaganda is one of America's most useful tools when sending out messages to the masses. Public lynchings in the late 1800s and early 1900s were used as a method to maintain racial conformity by terrorizing and instilling fear in Black Americans. Black Americans during these times would be lynched for "criminal accusations," which led to lynch mobs putting them to death without legal sanction, hanging them from trees, burning, dismembering the bodies, taking pieces of the bodies home for souvenirs. They took pictures, smiling in front of the hanging and burning Black bodies, and sold photos as souvenirs, too. They invited their friends and family; it was a tradition, a celebration for them. These murders could have easily been private affairs, but they were public for one reason only—to showcase what will happen to you, if you are Black and choose to challenge White supremacy in the slightest fashion, which could be something as simple as acknowledging the beauty in being Black.

Ida B. Wells, a Black woman journalist who was born into slavery, documented the horrifying practice of Black lynchings in the late 1890s. In 1892, three of Ida B. Wells's close friends, Thomas Moss, Will Stewart, and Calvin McDowell, were charged with "maintaining a public nuisance" after protecting The

People's Grocery in Memphis from an armed and racist White mob. In the middle of the night, a mob of seventy-five Whites seized the three friends from the jail, drove them away from the city, and beat and shot them to death. This was the straw that broke the camel's back—and what sparked Ida B. Wells to challenge the White power structure, which she did by dedicating her life to bring awareness and to combat lynchings in the South. She documented the lynchings and White mob violence through pictures and collected statistics, which we know today as "data journalism." Wells started a newspaper, *Free Speech*, that was attacked and burned by a White mob in May 1892. In 1893 and 1894, she traveled to England on a speaking tour, attending public meetings and forums to showcase what lynchings looked like in the American South. In 1894, she returned to America to continue her speaking tour. She published a book in 1895, *A Red Record: Tabulated Statistics and Alleged Causes of Lynchings in the United States.*

Anyone who takes it upon themselves to fight the White power structure in America is a courageous individual in my eyes. Ida B. Wells's work was important, revolutionary, and a step forward in the right direction toward Black liberation. She brought awareness to the brutal and violent history of White mobs and lynchings in America, conditions that some people may not have ever known existed in the South if it weren't for Wells. I understand the revolution in antilynching campaigns, and even the current campaigns that people have around anti-police brutality, and even gun violence in Black communities. However, for me, it's depressing being forced to see pictures and videos of people who look just like me and my loved ones get tortured and murdered. I know firsthand what getting stomped out by cops feels like. I still hear the sounds of screams in my nightmares from mothers mourning their dead child. I don't need to see videos of Black boys and girls getting murdered to know that Baltimore has roughly 300+ homicides a year—I live here, I walk the streets, I feel it. I don't need to see bloody bodies on the concrete to believe that it's going on, because I know. The Thanksgiving table shrinks in size. The slain don't pull up to the cookouts anymore. Friends in your group photos start to vanish. They won't be screaming congratulations when you're due to walk across the stage on graduation. The numbers you have saved for them in your phone will never ping again. I believe that Ida B. Wells knew that she had to go abroad and speak the truth, because the people in the South were dealing with the lynchings, being threatened and murdered by the noose. Why would they need pictures if they could smell the strange fruit hanging from the trees?

Ida B. Wells's plan to bring awareness to lynchings in the South was strategic and effective. I believe that sharing videos and images of trauma can be effective, but I believe there needs to be a more strategic approach, than just aimlessly sharing the images and videos on social media with no direction. I have noticed that when some people post traumatic videos, they'll have some type of disclaimer or trigger warning, letting the viewer know that the content can be sensitive. Every Black experience in America isn't the same. I know some Black people who have never lost a friend or family member to violence. I know some Black people that never had physical altercations with police, or even grew up loving cops. So their relationship to viral content of murders and police brutality might be different from that of someone who's been directly affected.

Any activist or pillar of the community will tell you that you have to keep one foot in the revolution, and one foot out, and if not, it has the potential to drive you mad. Nowadays because we are stuck to our phones, and have unlimited access to breaking news globally, I believe that it's harder to keep that one foot out of the revolution, when the harsh realities of racism are hunting you down—constantly being shoved in your face. During the years when there were no cell phones, if you wanted access to news, statistics, videos, and images of police violence, you had to actively seek it. Now because we have cell phones, the racist propaganda and the "support" of Black Lives Matter are in the palm of our hands.

Being Black in America and watching agents of the state torture and murder Black people every day, and being forced to watch because it is so ubiquitous, is a psychological media tactic to cause fear and terror and high ratings. When the media highlights White supremacist like Dylan Roof, who killed nine Black churchgoers in Charleston, South Carolina, and was taken to Burger King hours after his arrest because he hadn't eaten, it sends a message. George Zimmerman went free after murdering Trayvon Martin in Florida and later sold the gun he used to kill Trayvon at a gun show for $138,900. From the Black people being killed, to Whites not being held accountable for the killings, all of it is propaganda to maintain racial conformity and takes a continuous psychological toll.

According to the Equal Justice Initiative, of all lynchings committed after 1900, only 1 percent resulted in a lyncher being convicted of a criminal offense of any kind: "The vast majority of lynching participants were never punished, both because of the tacit approval of law enforcement, and because dozens if not hundreds often had a hand in the killing. Still, punishment was not unheard of—though most of the time, if white lynchers were tried or convicted, it was for arson, rioting, or some other much more minor offense."[1]

---

1 Equal Justice Initiative, https://eji.org/.

Again, I believe that the public display of this trauma can work with a strategy and intent of teaching those who might be unaware, not just aimlessly sharing on the Internet. I believe that this is ideal and the safest approach. One of the most historic public displays of the Black male corpse happened in Chicago at Roberts Temple Church of God in Christ in 1955.

In the summer of 1955, Emmett Till, a fourteen-year-old boy from Chicago, had traveled to Mississippi to visit relatives. One day, Till stopped at Bryant's Grocery and Meat Market, not knowing his trip would be a death sentence. Carolyn Bryant, the White woman who was behind the counter, claimed that Till wolf-whistled and said, "Bye Baby," as he walked out of the store. Carolyn told her brother, J.W. Milam, and husband, Roy Bryant, what Till did, and days later after returning from a business trip, the two went to Till's great-uncle's house. They dragged Till out of the house, and they beat, shot, and murdered him. They wrapped barbed wire and tied a seventy-five-pound cotton gin fan to his neck, and dumped his lifeless body in the Tallahatchie River. The two White men were acquitted after the jury deliberated for less than an hour. Till's face was beyond recognition when his bloated body was found. Law enforcement wanted to bury Till's body hours after it was retrieved. Emmett Till's mother, Mammie Till Bradley, was distraught by what those White men did to her son. She said, "Let the people see what they did to my boy," and held an open casket funeral that had 100,000 visitors. Images of Till's ravaged body were posted everywhere from *Jet* magazine, to other media outlets and news. His mother forced the public to reckon with the brutal reality of racism in this country and wanted the world to see what White supremacy can look like at its highest form. The image of Till's body, the White men not getting arrested for killing him—even after admitting to the murder in an interview—and the nature of his death added steam to the Civil Rights movement—and publicized what was wrong with America.

While Carolyn Bryant was on her death bed, six decades later, she admitted that her claims of Emmett whistling at her and touching her were all a lie. There are countless others who have blood on their hands, without even getting them dirty, and the sad part is that we'll never know how many Black lives they've destroyed.

It reminds us who this country is, what we've done, and what we have the capability to do. That's why when people discuss the White woman, Amy Cooper, who called the police on the Black male, Christian Cooper, in Central Park on May 25, 2020, and explicitly stated that he is African American, I can't help but think of the thousands of Black males who have been jailed, beaten, murdered, and lynched just because some white women didn't want them in their space—some under the same exact accusations as with Emmett Till.

What Mamie Till did was courageous. She brought awareness to an issue that's been on the forefront of Black American minds for the longest time. The sacrifice she made for the world was something that many people wouldn't do. Think about the agony she faced her entire life. She knew what her baby looked liked before his demise, she saw him in the casket, she wouldn't have been able to erase the image even if she wanted to. But not only that, she had to see it in the paper, magazines, and other places promoting the brutal history of America.

The Black male corpse, and the death of the Black male, are always used to make statements, and to show the world the injustices going on in America. Images of dead Black people have been and still are one of America's methods of propaganda to promote racial conformity, and its harsh realities. They can be used as ammo, and as hype for racists to see, love, and crow over our deaths. But another harsh reality is that today, we who share those videos are doing the job of perpetuating the racial spectacle by constantly posting and sharing images of Black injustices, and a fine line develops between raising awareness and stoking that spectacle. It's these images of police brutality that are finally exposing, for all Americans and the world at large, what is happening in our streets and homes. But again, the spectacle is lamentable.

Even when race isn't involved, being in constant reminder and seeing public displays of death, tragedy, and even mourning can cause harm. Earlier this year we lost Kobe Bryant and his daughter Gianna in a helicopter crash. Kobe being one of the greatest and most popular basketball players to ever live, and his daughter being a basketball player, too, I'm pretty sure they had billions of people mourning their deaths. Many of those mourners took their feelings to Instagram, not fully understanding how this would harm Vanessa and Natalia Bryant, Kobe's wife and younger daughter. During this time, the two made their Instagram pages private, and blocked the Kobe and Gianna fan pages, to keep others from reposting their pictures. "This makes it 10x harder to deal with our loss. We hope that people understand that although these fan pages have good intentions, they make moving forward harder since they are constant reminders," wrote Natalia in her Instagram story. Vanessa made a similar statement: "I have unfortunately had to block fan pages because it's been really hard to go online and constantly see pics of our beloved Gigi and Kobe under every single square of our explore pages. . . . We [love] you all but please understand that we had to do this for our own healing not because we don't appreciate your [love]."

If it's losing a loved one to a freak accident, or to police brutality or gun violence, seeing excessive images and videos of those tragedies has the ability to take a toll on anyone's mental health.

People like myself don't have the luxury to take ourselves

out of "harmful" environments, because it's where we make a living, eat, take care of our families, go to school, and repeat. We can't hit the block button on real life. We can't change the factory settings of our lives to "private," when crooked cops disguised as public servants terrorize us daily.

I can't help but question whether I am an accomplice as racist White Americans carry out their propaganda mission to instill fear, continue racial conformity, and keep us in check, by sharing the videos. Am I aiding in the propaganda of racists romanticizing Black death? Racist don't have to go out and take pictures of burning and mutilated Black bodies, because we do it. They don't have to hold celebrations and ceremonies around lynchings, because they can kick back in the comforts of their homes, eat casserole and popcorn, drink champagne, invite other racists friends and family over, and watch us die on their phone screens. Why should racists do the work, when we can do it for them? Remember, that they want us to feel like and be seen as victims, because again, lynchings could have easily been a private savagery ceremony for racist Whites, but they chose to make them public. The public slayings of Black men should not be the backbone of "moving in the right direction," when it comes to race relations in this country.

Haven't we had enough? Do we—one nation under God— need to see yet another and another public slaying of a Black man or woman to keep "moving in the right direction" when it comes to race relations? These spectacles should not be counted on to keep sparking our passions whenever there is a lull in interest and activism around racial issues. We as a nation don't need to see any more shootings, any more knees on necks, any more murders. We've been immersed in these visuals. Our focus must remain steadfast and resolute on dialogue and action to ensure that the violence ends.

If Peach Fuzz Could Talk

I was sitting outside of a cruddy vacant home across the street from Canaan Missionary Baptist Church, waiting on my little brother Tuane to come meet me. His best friend, who was also like a little brother to me, Poody, was murdered a week before, and this day was his funeral. Tuane pulled up after twenty minutes of me being out here alone. He pulled up with vodka inside of an Everfresh bottle and a pack of Black & Milds, and we embalmed our bodies with the poison to suffocate our feelings, until it was time to enter the church. Poody was nineteen years old and was loved by the people in his neighborhood, and I got to see a glimpse of the young father he was coming to be, leaving behind his baby boy.

I always dread going to funerals—yes because it's emotional, but honestly, it's the preachers for me. Plain and simple, they just be lying too much. The same children that they call thugs 364 days out of the year are now angels with hearts of gold on the day of their funeral because they're getting a check. The old folks are always semiannoying with their Bengay-scented clothes and the smell of Newports busting out of their mouths— and they're always saying things like "Oh my God, baby. You've grown so much since the last time I saw you." As if the last time they didn't see me were when I was ten.

Every funeral I've ever attended in the past of someone who was slain, I always think about life-threatening situations that I've barely made it out of.

You ever heard of six degrees of separation? It's the idea that everyone is six or even fewer social connections away from one another. It's sometimes even referred to as the six hand-shakes rule. Baltimore? It's more like two degrees.

The summer sun was fat and bright on this particular day, I had to be around twelve or thirteen. Me and my homeboys decided to go swimming at Patterson Park's pool, which was a summertime ritual for us. We attended the pool at least three to five times a week. The pool experience wasn't fun if you didn't break the rules. We'd run over all of the "walk," signs painted on the ground, diving and doing flips in the "no diving" sec-tions of the pool, and ignoring the lifeguard's whistles. We never brought towels with us, because we'd dry off on the walk back home, talking about how we're gonna inhale turkey sandwiches, potato chips, and Hawaiian Punch once we got back to the block. On this particular day, we arrived at the park but never made it to the pool.

Me and my homies all shared one bicycle, and we called it "the block bike." If someone needed to use the block bike to make a store run, or had to visit a friend, it was there for you. Block bikes get trashed and traded in quickly for others because they are always throwaway material—beat-up frame, mis-matched colored wheels, faulty brakes, if any brakes at all, and chipped paint. The block bike always stayed outside and wasn't brought into anyone's home, so it could be accessible to every-one. We felt comfortable doing this because the majority of my friends and I lived on the same block, and the ones who didn't, you would've thought they did because of how much they were around. At this point, our block bike had been missing for a few days, and when we arrived at the park, we saw the dude Shawn on it, who was not a friend of ours, or part of our clique. Off the bat we didn't accuse Shawn, because it's normal for people to steal things, and let others borrow, not letting them know its stolen. That still wasn't going to stop us from making Shawn aware that he was on our bike, and we needed it back.

We made our way to Shawn, and I said, "Yo, where you get that bike from? You know that's our shit, right?" In the calmest tone.

Shawn responded, "What the fuck y'all talkn' bout? This my bike. Y'all niggas really wanna beef over a bike!?" As if he were trying to scream his eyeballs out of his sockets.

Me and my homies looked at one another, trying to decide if we should just beat his ass in front of everyone out there. I had no doubt in my mind, that's the reason he was showing off in the first place because of how embarrassing it was for an eighteen-year-old to get pressed by thirteen-year-olds in front of a crowd of people.

My homie Rece said, "Yo, Shawn, you ain't gotta do all of that, we just tryna get our shi—"

Shawn cut Rece off midsentence, "Man, fuck y'all! What y'all tryna do!?" still screaming.

Rece handed me his phone, took his shirt off, and asked Shawn, "Yo, what you wanna fight? You could've just said that off rip."

Shawn stiffened like a broomstick, because he knew that getting physical with Rece wasn't a smart move. A week or so prior to this day, Rece demonstrated how lethal his hands were after beating up one of Shawn's friends, Quille, who started a beef with Rece because he disliked the fact he was dating his sister—a bunch of bullshit that could've been avoided if I'm being honest. Shawn declined Rece's offer by screaming, "I be right back, I got something for you niggas," as he peeled off on the bike, heading toward South Linwood Avenue. Unless you have a pistol on you, or one in close proximity, and someone says, "I be right back," you never wait on their return, because they'll have a gun with them. We left the park and headed back toward the block and were talking about how much of a clown and sucker Shawn was, especially for going to get a gun for some children. Still on our journey to the block, we halted at the corner of Glover Street and Fayette Street, waiting for traffic to stop so we could cross. THUMP THUMP THUMP, we heard footsteps behind us and turned around. It was Shawn using his feet for brakes on the bike. "Oh, y'all wanna beef over a bike," he said, trying to yank the pistol out of his jeans. We turned back around, scattered, and I heard "click click, click, click," his gun was jammed. Everyone ran in different directions, and one of my homies even hopped in the bed of a pickup truck that was in motion. I wasn't friends with Shawn; however, that same hand that pulled a gun out on me was the same hand that I shook at a Chuck E. Cheese Party some years ago. Remember I told you that Baltimore was small? Shawn was a blood relative of my younger brother Fidel. It wouldn't make me and Shawn blood, because Fidel and I have the same father, different mothers.

It was just our luck that the next day Rece and his brothers had to play in a basketball tournament at an outdoor court, located a few blocks from where we lived, but smack dab in the middle of Shawn's stomping grounds. We knew that something could've popped off, but we all decided to go anyway. Twenty minutes into the game, Shawn pulls up on the bike, on the opposite side of the gate where the games were being held. Next to him was one of his homeboys, who he handed the bike over to.

His homeboy rode the bike over to a pile of trash bags in an alley, reached in, and pulled out a pistol—tucking it in his waistband. I couldn't tell if it was the same strap that Shawn had the day before, but I was thinking, what if it doesn't jam this time? We were tense the entire tournament but felt no need to run because at that stage in our lives we believed that there was no such thing in ducking murder. We believed if something was going to happen, then it was just gonna happen.

The tournament ended with everyone going home unharmed. The evening consisted of mean-mugs, and constant grabbing of waistbands, and basketball. I look back at this incident and think about how desensitized we were to violent murders. We knew that these guys had bullets with our names on them but still placed ourselves in a position to get hurt. Violence has been a norm, since we were babies—we was born in it, molded by it. Almost as if we were inviting to the trauma.

I sipped more of my vodka on the steps of the cruddy vacant home and passed it to my little brother as we made our way to the church entrance. It felt like a Friday night how packed Poody's funeral was. Tears and screams controlling the room, people passing out, kids crying and saying how much they miss their big brother—and the preacher, lying, just making me wish that I had more vodka. I walked up to the casket and stared at Poody, looking at the peach fuzz on his face. Thinking about all of the other babies in suits I had to lay eyes on. Thinking about how this country never gave him a fair chance. He didn't even get to experience adulthood, and what it would have to offer him. I was standing there thinking again, how I would have looked inside of the casket, if Shawn's gun didn't jam. What would my funeral have looked like? How my family would've had to go into debt or scrape up funds to bury a body that they used to pray for— prayers that hardly ever seemed to be heard. Violent murders are always untimely. Even if there's a dark cloud lingering over a person, you never truly know when it's going to storm.

Statista reported that in 2019, the market size of funeral homes in the US was over 16.8 billion US dollars.[1] According to the National Funeral Directors Association (NFDA), the median price for a funeral including embalming, a casket, a viewing, and a burial costs $7,000 to $8,000.[2] After contacting March Funeral Homes in Baltimore, I was told that the average cost is $6,600.

Spending money that you don't have and going into debt is commonplace for poor Black people in America. I know families who had to put liens on their homes, borrow money, take out loans, and start GoFundMes just to bury their loved ones. In a country where capitalism sucks the energy, blood, and soul out of individuals, especially in poor communities, no one has thousands of dollars lying around for a funeral. Aside from the financial debt—that person who died used to be an extra source of income to keep bread on the table—we suffer from emotional, mental, and spiritual debts, as well.

I'm still at Poody's funeral, just thinking about how I was never taught about death and the big business behind it. No one taught us anything close to understanding how violence in our communities was related to racism. All we were told was to try and "stay out of the way," which is impossible when you live in the middle of the chaos. We were also told to pray, which became our safety net. Prayer is a home base we can slide to when things are good or bad. You want that dream job, then

---

1   Mazareanu, E. "Market size of funeral homes in the United States from 2015 to 2020." Statista, April 3, 2020, https://www.statista.com/statistics /883227/revenue-of-funeral-homes-in-the-us/.

2   National Funeral Directors Association, https://www.nfda.org/news /statistics.

pray. Your homie is laid up in the hospital suffering from gun-shot wounds, you pray. There's not a song that's sung in heaven powerful enough to stop the violence that goes on in my city. No one told me that prayers, psalms, or songs can't shield Black bodies from bullets.

I'm sitting in the funeral asking myself, what's the point of voting new people into office, if it doesn't matter, because bullets run this town? The bullets wear the pants in Baltimore's political relationship. We need to realize that prayers don't stop violence, but antiracist laws, policies, and ideas are what have the ability to stop violence. I can't count how many times I felt stranded in a dark tunnel, and I prayed to God. I asked God to give me an exit strategy that I could follow—I prayed for him to show me the light. You see the light at the end of the tunnel, only to realize that it's not a way out, but the light is just another train coming.

Every chance I get I have to bring awareness to gun vio-lence, and the effects it has on people like myself who come from similar communities. Zora Neale Hurston once wrote, "If you are silent about your pain, they'll kill you and say you enjoyed it." There's no way that I can be silent.

My Home Is a
Noiseless Gun

List of things that go on at my home: Cruddy stuff. Sad stuff. The things-nobody-can-help stuff, and good stuff. My home is a noiseless gun: it fires, but there is no sonic boom of the bullet. After someone is hit, the silence confuses the minds of the victims and the bystanders, tricking them into believing that the previous traumatic event(s) "weren't so bad."

My home is a kiss. And sometimes when it puckers its lips, it electrifies. My home is warm, but when the temperature rises and the heat slithers from around the corner, we scatter. We run toward it. We're from Baltimore, so we two-step in the fire. And boy oh boy, those flames cause us to look worn-out like burnt scriptures, while we are still wet behind the ears. It's like we go from age ten to twenty-one in three to five business days. The children who grow up fast are clear-cut reflections of a troubled past, and a tip-off for an idiosyncratic future. My home loves, but it loves different. It loves us the only way it knows how.

Out front, local rap music hisses from foreign cars. Gold chains draped over naked pubescent torsos, the word "Loyalty"

137

inscribed in ink and blood over the heart. Despite the fact that Granny said, "You better not get no tattoos on your arm if you want a good job in the future." A tattoo is the least of your worries; "good jobs" won't spot your ink because applicants who carry the names Tyrone and Darius are never interviewed.

Children landing double back somersaults on charred pissy mattresses that have steel coils and foam bursting through the fabric. Mattress + street = somebody got put out for not paying their rent. One man's unpaid bills become another man's playground. Kids from the hood are little alchemists, always turning lead into gold.

This brick-red row home is mine. That blue sticky spot cluttered with flies is where my little brother spilled his soda. Some bleach and hot water will get it out. That's a flowerpot—it just ain't got no flowers in it. Only dirt and piled-up trash that all of us disobedient kids slam-dunked into it. That old man with titties, propped out of that window across the street? That's Mr. Luke. He's nosy, and a gossip. He tells my grandmother every little thing. I remember I had thrown a marble at a speeding car on Orleans Street. I sprinted home, and by the time I stretched open the screen door, my grandmother was there holding a leather strap, with the face of a devil sick of sin. "Mr. Luke told me—" is all I remember before my grandmother went Lara Croft on my ass.

That banister is almost always broken, so don't grab on it too hard, or at all. Everything that goes on the other side of this peephole is where I lay my head.

This house is a hub for outlaw lovemaking, which we call "doing it." I be doing it, my lil brother be doing it, my cousin be doing it, and I have factual evidence that my mother always be doing it. She has the kids, the miscarriages, and the abortion receipts to prove it.

This house is a capital for drug abuse, which is always disguised as a "celebration." I never knew what was there to celebrate. But then again, in life, what doesn't kill you makes you go crazy. Nobody blasted themselves today. Let's party!

Bent empty cans of Steele Reserve 211 overflow the grocery bags hanging on door knobs. You might find a clear capsule with heroin residue tucked under the baseboard. You may also find a "love rose," which are roses in small glass tubes that are sold at corner stores in my neighborhood, intended as gifts for your sweetheart. But the love was gone once that rose was plucked out and replaced with a pregnant rock of crack, steel wool, and a lighter flame, hence the burn marks, which births a new romance more sacred than rice rain and cake cutting.

That's my grandmother on the couch. Her only exercise is raising cigarettes and cups of coffee to her lips, cursing out her disorderly grandkids, chasing Facebook on her cell phone, and flipping through channels for the next NFL or NBA game.

If you walk down these steps, it leads you to the kitchen. Yes, our kitchen is in the basement. Watch your feet and make sure you don't step on any sticky pads. There are two mice in here that we can't catch for nothing. My grandmother says only dirty people have mice in their homes. Them mice in here come from the lady next door.

That's my aunt at the sink committing a homicide on my lil cousin's naps with a hot comb, sounding like sizzling chicken and shrimp from TGI Friday's. You haven't been to Hell until someone puts that "Just For Me" perm stuff in your head. I've seen my lil cousin cry just looking at that jar.

If you look past my cousin, you'll see a khaki-colored dinted door. If you turn the knob, it'll take you outside.

This is our backyard. A concrete square of endless amusement and scattered rat poop. No matter how much we sweep, it always returns. This is where me and my homeboys have amateur crap games where we shoot the five and bet the ten. Crooked smiles crowded with gold teeth blowing on dice, wishing for new tennis shoes. Whenever me and my friends got into arguments, this becomes a boxing arena where egos get mangled. That crate hanging by old strings from the balcony is what we used for a basketball rim.

Cookouts? Oh, we don't throw cookouts back here. The cookouts throw us. The cookouts throw us into contemplation about punching the clock or calling out of our night shift. The cookouts throw us into bottles of Advil and Budweiser. The next morning, attempting to hang the hangover. The cookouts are the puppeteers—we are on the strings. We forgive them for the stabbing pain in our kidneys, the vomiting, and the headaches, then allow them to throw us, again.

If you look up from here, you'll see our metal gray balcony where at times I loom over and watch the sun sink. When the darkness barged in, this alleyway is where uncanny accidents occurred. People getting robbed at fist-point. Naked women running with urine dribbling down their thighs. Junkies spitting out blood through their last two incisors. I heard this one lady yell at this guy, "You never do shit for the damn kids." That's what she said right before she landed hawk spit directly into his eye. Neither me nor him saw that coming.

If there are people delighted after visiting my home, then I am glad. If they are not, then it doesn't matter. Some would argue that there is more love in the dead arms of an enemy than what's at my home. But, angels don't always sing. The sun doesn't shine in Heaven, all the time. Paradise wouldn't be who she truly is if she never experienced a little pain. My home loves, but it loves different. It loves us the only way it knows how.

* * *

Our crown has already been bought and paid for.
All we have to do is wear it.
—James Baldwin

For the women in my neighborhood who wore pink and blue hair when the whole world called it "ghetto." For the young men who got face tattoos and gift-wrapped their teeth with gold and diamonds before it was trendy, when people pinned it as "unprofessional," "gang-related," and "ghetto." For the ones who wheelie'd pedal bikes through traffic and were called "reckless," instead of being hailed for their talent. For all of the young Black pioneers who were brave enough to wear their hoods on their back and rep their cities like gangs, despite the world's criticism. For the ones who have been the leading scorers on setting pop culture trends but don't get the credit from mainstream media— not that they want it, nor seek it, but it should be known. This for y'all. This is for us.

Majority of my childhood, and well into my teenage years, my grandmother, along with other friends and family who belonged to my community, often told me, "I don't want you end up like them niggas." "Them niggas" who pocket pistols in preparation for civil wars amongst their neighbors. Who fail math in school but know numbers when a brick of coke is involved, "them niggas." "Them niggas" with hunchbacks who stand as if the world were glued to their shoulder blades. Whose mean mugs be two-ton, who have deep stories of anger loaded in their laugh lines. "Them niggas" with mile-long mouths who scream "fuck the police" as they bend corners in squad cars. "Them niggas" who stay within a three-mile radius of where they live, until they die. Who only attend church for funeral services but inscribe bible scriptures in ink and blood on their bodies, "them niggas." "Them niggas" who collect baby mamas like tennis shoes. Who stand on the block for hours and crack: crack jokes, crack open liquor bottles, slang crack, crack jaws when somebody cracks slick, "them niggas." "Them niggas" who rock cruddy fades tall enough for five heads. "Them niggas," who say "Baldamore," instead of "Baltimore." If you ain't none of "them niggas," then you're guilty by association, my grandmother strongly believed. My grandmother wanted to make sure that I would be as little of "them niggas," and as much "American" as possible. Because the more "American" I was, the more I'd be ready for "the real world," meaning, I believe, the "White world," because obviously I wouldn't be successful at life if I was one of "them niggas."

"You better not put none of them damn fronts in your mouth, I paid too much money for them braces," my grandmother yelled from the kitchen, located in the basement. Me and my friend had both just gotten summer jobs and were discussing what we are going to spend our first checks on, and my grandmother was eavesdropping. Little did she know that no power in this universe was gonna stop me from getting six of my teeth covered in gold. She was also a few days late, because I had already been fitted and was scheduled to pick them up from Golden Brothers, a jewelry store in downtown Baltimore the following week.

Getting your first pair of fronts is a rite of passage to Baltimoreans located on the Eastside, a.k.a. "Down Da Hill." Getting your first tattoo was a rite of passage, as well; I had gotten mine a year prior. I was told tattoos make people look "ignorant," and that if I got any, I wouldn't get a "good job" in the "future." At this point in my life, there wasn't an adult, not even my grandmother, whose words held sway over my decision making. Back around the time when I was thirteen, I knew what I wanted: I got my first ink in the basement of a guy named Rell, who didn't require parental supervision while tattooing minors.

On my right arm was a cross, with "R.I.P." above it and "Fidel" below. That was my little brother, who died in a house fire at seven years old. Inscribing a loved one's name in your flesh is ritual, one of the many ways we honor our fallen.

"You need to stop wearing all them damn tennis shoes and big-ass shirts. You need some real clothes," my grandmother would say. Real clothes were dress shoes and button-up shirts, as if I were attending Bible study every day. Imagine being the only kid on the block dressed in loafers, slacks, and Oxford shirts. In Baltimore City? Yeah, right. I would've spent the majority of my childhood fighting off jokesters. Then imagine how upset my grandmother would've been at me, scuffling on the streets every day, getting those fancy clothes she paid for dirty.

"If you don't listen to me you're gonna end up like your mother and father." My grandmother made it known that my parents' heroin habits and their frequent stays in prison happened because they didn't listen to my grandmother or their elders. My grandmother, on the other hand, was the backbone of our family because she had listened to her guardians and had gotten herself educated. And no less than that is what she wanted for and from me.

Neither my grandmother nor I was a scholar when it came to understanding the influence environments have on physical, mental, and moral development. We didn't know that we were brainwashed to accept White value systems and White standards of beauty, which made us trade in our eyes for a new pair that only sees a monster when we look in the mirror. And new sets of lips that might not ever utter the words "Black is beautiful." We didn't know that "good education" in schools did not teach Black people to deal with life how we must face it. My grandmother always stayed on top of me and my "education," and I maintained good grades. I could pass a math exam. I was great at spelling. I was trained my entire life on how to do well in school on paper, but not in life. My family and friends didn't create this culture, it was handed over to us like hand-me-down coats. Even if they were too big, we still wore them on our shoulder blades.

Just like every other group in this country, we are on a journey to find success. We are on a journey to learn, and grow, and to see what this country has in store for us, and to find ways that we can pass down the heirlooms we've attained to our loved ones, with the hopes of making their journey less difficult than it was for those who came before them. A part of being antiracist is that we have to first acknowledge our racist ideas and stereotypes that we have about other groups, throw them away, and our newfound antiracist ideas should be reflected in our actions—through the policies we support, the literature we teach our children, the way we treat people on the street, etc. This is not the be-all and end-all, but it is a means that will point us in the right direction.

There is nothing wrong with Black people, or with any other racial group. And if you insist that one racial group has to be "more American" (code for White American) in order to live a life with freedom, happiness, and dignity, then a first step is to understand that that is a racist idea. Racist ideas undermine and devalue our shared humanity, whereas antiracist ideas, perspectives, and resulting actions value and respect cultural and physical differences among and within all racial groups. These differences should not threaten anyone's freedoms in this country or anywhere.

Acknowledgments

I'd like to thank my editor Hector Carosso for giving me the space to spread my wings while writing this book, but also pushing me to the limits, which revealed parts of me that I never knew existed. Britney Crawford, my manager, has been there for me—supportive since we first met—and is always pushing me to reach newer heights. I'm grateful for my agent Latoya C. Smith, who believed in me and took a chance on me when no one else did. Can't wait to see what the future holds for us in the literary world.

My undergraduate English Professor Arnold Westbrook is who engaged me in literature, which sparked my writing interest. It's hard to think what my life would be like without his influence. Every interaction I have with Dr. Zoe Spencer leaves me a better person and thinker. She took me under her wing, constantly nourishing me with her expertise and experiences. The Nu Psi Chapter of Omega Psi Phi Fraternity Incorporated are my brothers, and I'm honored to be a part of the organization. Through their teachings, I learned the importance of time management, leaving zero room for excuses, and starting what you finish—some core principles that helped me during the process of writing this book.

Dr. Ibram X. Kendi's dedication to telling the truth about this country's ugly history and present is what made me grow stronger in my antiracism work. He is a gem to us all. My former manager Kerry Graham—I want to thank her for the countless hours we've spent together in the past reading, writing, and discussing education and ways to combat racism using literature.

All of the grade school teachers and professors who put my work in their curriculums played a vital role in my journey, because without them, I wouldn't have established relationships with such great academic institutions and students.

Ninety five percent of this book, I wrote while staying at Hotel Revival in Baltimore. I never thought that I'd fall in love with a hotel, but the general manager Donte Johnson and his staff did a wonderful job at making me feel as if I were home.

My big brother D. Watkins encouraged me to start writing essays a few years ago, and I couldn't be more thankful for where his mentorship has lead me. My sister Valencia D. Clay helped me see that "Love is all around us, we just gotta look for it." I'm grateful for all of our conversations where we explored life's deep questions. Wallace Lane, thank you for always looking through the barebones of writings I send you—your feedback has been a large part of my development as a writer over the past few years. D, Valencia, and Wallace are three people who asked me vital questions that lead to essential answers while writing this book.

My cousin Avon Bryant has been my source of uplift and direction since we were children, and as adults, nothing has changed. He answers my calls and pulls up whenever I need him, just as he did through the writing of this book.

My Gemini brother and best friend Devin Allen gave me

the best foreword I could ever ask for. His honesty, his resilience, and dedication to his work and to the people of Baltimore keeps me inspired day in and day out.

Gail and Mary, my two grandmothers, made sacrifices and contributions that greatly benefited our family. If it wasn't for them, I wouldn't be the man that I am today. Through all of the good, bad, and ugly, I am grateful for both of my parents, Fuzzy and Mo, for providing my DNA, and being some of the realest people I ever met. My family has always protected me the best way that they knew how, and it paid off.

Fidel (rest in peace), Antuane, Rashad, Ronald, Ka'Maya, Ka'Mary, and Tenise. My beautiful younger siblings are always at the forefront of my mind when making life-changing decisions. Every day I strive to become a better person so they can have a positive role model to follow.

Shout out to all of my angels who watch over me and guide me. Fidel, Davon, Deek, Dee Dave, Great Granny Virginia, Poody, Trav, Ty, Fresh, and the countless others.

Lastly, I want to thank God for all of the blessings he's given me in life, including everyone that I mentioned above, and the ones who didn't get mentioned, that played a part of my development. Forever.

READER'S NOTES

READER'S NOTES

READER'S NOTES

_____
_____
_____
_____
_____
_____
_____
_____
_____
_____
_____
_____
_____
_____
_____
_____
_____
_____
_____
_____
_____
_____
_____
_____
_____
_____
_____

READER'S NOTES

READER'S NOTES

READER'S NOTES

READER'S NOTES

READER'S NOTES

_____
_____
_____
_____
_____
_____
_____
_____
_____
_____
_____
_____
_____
_____
_____
_____
_____
_____
_____
_____
_____
_____
_____
_____
_____
_____
_____
_____
_____

READER'S NOTES

_____
_____
_____
_____
_____
_____
_____
_____
_____
_____
_____
_____
_____
_____
_____
_____
_____
_____
_____
_____
_____
_____
_____
_____
_____
_____
_____
_____

READER'S NOTES

_____
_____
_____
_____
_____
_____
_____
_____
_____
_____
_____
_____
_____
_____
_____
_____
_____
_____
_____
_____
_____
_____
_____
_____
_____
_____
_____

READER'S NOTES

READER'S NOTES

READER'S NOTES

READER'S NOTES

READER'S NOTES

_____
_____
_____
_____
_____
_____
_____
_____
_____
_____
_____
_____
_____
_____
_____
_____
_____
_____
_____
_____
_____
_____
_____
_____
_____
_____
_____
_____

READER'S NOTES

READER'S NOTES

READER'S NOTES

_____
_____
_____
_____
_____
_____
_____
_____
_____
_____
_____
_____
_____
_____
_____
_____
_____
_____
_____
_____
_____
_____
_____
_____
_____
_____
_____

READER'S NOTES

READER'S NOTES